# In Ordinary Time

# In Ordinary Time

HEALING THE WOUNDS OF THE HEART

Roberta C. Bondi

ABINGDON PRESS
*Nashville*

IN ORDINARY TIME
HEALING THE WOUNDS OF THE HEART

*Copyright © 1996 by Abingdon Press*

*This book is printed on recycled, acid-free paper.*

**Library of Congress Cataloging-in-Publication Data**

Bondi, Roberta C.
In ordinary time: healing the wounds of the heart/Roberta C. Bondi.
    p.   cm.
Includes bibliographical references.
ISBN 0-687-27326-9 (alk. paper)
1. Prayer—Christianity.   I. Title.
BV215.B59   1996
248.3'2—dc20

96-16772
CIP

**Illustrations by John Boegel**

96 97 98 99 00 01 02 03 04 05 — 10 9 8 7 6 5 4 3 2 1

MANUFACTURED IN THE UNITED STATES OF AMERICA

# ◊ C O N T E N T S ◊

# ◊ P R E F A C E ◊

Prayer is a hard topic for most of us modern folk, and we have little place to talk about it. My own first conversation partners were the great ancient teachers, the Abbas and Ammas of the Egyptian desert whose sayings now appear in English primarily in *The Sayings of the Desert Fathers: The Alphabetical Collection*, translated by Benedicta Ward. These men and women have been urging me for nearly thirty years to pray and to seek healing for the wounds of my heart I carry from childhood, from my own temperament, from my culture, even the culture of my church. They have also urged me all along to write about what I have learned from them and from my own experience, for, as they tell us, nothing, neither the most wonderful nor the most humiliating thing we are given as Christians, is ever given for ourselves alone.[1] To them above all, I am grateful for help, encouragement, and goading for the writing of this book.

The chapters that follow are in the form of letters to a friend. My intention, of course, is that you, the reader, understand yourself to be the friend to whom I am writing, and certainly this is more than a literary fiction. I have received so many letters myself over the years asking what I think about just the topics I write of here, and I have so many faces before my eyes as I write, faces of people I know well, faces of those I've briefly met only once, and imagined faces of other people I've never met at all but to whom I still feel very attached. I thank you, the reader, for providing me the impetus for these letters.

I also want to thank Bobbi Patterson, my friend and longtime modern conversation partner in prayer, particularly; much of the middle three chapters was written specifically under the inspiration of her friendship. Agatha Zwillig, O.S.B., and Mary Reuter, O.S.B., two of the most

---

1. *To Love as God Loves: Conversations with the Early Church* (Minneapolis: Augsburg-Fortress, 1987), and *To Pray and to Love: Conversations on Prayer with the Early Church* (Augsburg-Fortress, 1991); both are attempts to focus on what these great teachers of the early church have to teach us today.

faithful and loving correspondents I could imagine, were also present to me in a special way in this process.

As usual, I also relied heavily on the support of my dear friend Melissa Walker, and I was never disappointed.

I am grateful, too, to the following people for conversation about the project and/or reading parts of the manuscript: Bettie Banks, Cynthia Blakeley, Caroline Bynum, Tere Canzoneri, Rebecca Chopp, Pamela Couture, Betsy Fodor, Zora Ugolini Herr, Maggie Kulyk, John Mogabgab, Deborah Wight-Knight. Thanks to my many students at Candler who listen so well and so patiently, and ask such good questions.

I especially appreciate Nicole and John Mills's willingness to let me be there with them after their son Stefan's accident. It is of my own experience of the time that followed that I write in chapter 5.

I want to thank two communities, especially, for their support and nurture of me over the years. The first is the Emmaus Community, the ecumenical house church to which I belong. The other is that of the Sisters of St. Benedict in St. Joseph, Minnesota, where I am an oblate; over the years they have embodied for me in living form the monastic love, generous spirit, and enthusiasm for all things human that I first met in the ancient teachers I study.

Most particularly, I am grateful to my husband, Richard. His sensitive knowledge, judgment, cooking, and kindness to me seem sometimes almost without limits.

Finally, I thank my friends at Abingdon Press, but most especially my dear editor, Ulrike Guthrie; she has given me the benefit of extraordinary support, love, and care at every stage of the work.

## ◊ O N E ◊

# The Field We Grow In

*My dear friend,*

How good it was to get your letter today! It has been such a long time since I heard from you. I'm very glad to hear that you've come to a time when things are going pretty well in your life with your job and your family. After some of the things you've been through over the past few years, you deserve a little breathing room for a while.

You also say, however, that in spite of how well things are going around you, all of a sudden you find that the old stuff that hurt you in your childhood is rising up in you again, causing you trouble, and frustrating you. You ask me why I think it is happening now. Of course, I can't really tell you, but I can say that I have often noticed the same thing with me. It has often seemed as though I really couldn't get to some of the deeper things I needed to wrestle with until my external life (if there is such a thing!) was settled down enough that I could see what was going on inside me. Actually, this is a major reason why the early monastics I study left the former world they lived in to go out into the desert; without the stresses and distractions that came with just trying to make it in the world from one day to the next, it gave them a chance to confront what was really inside them.[1]

At any rate, I'm happy to hear that you've decided to begin to seek healing in your prayer for some of what is hurting you. You say in your letter that you know I have spent a lot of time over the years wrestling in my own prayer, seeking healing for the wounds of the heart that I carry myself. Now, you ask me, if you write to me with some questions that are arising for you, would I be willing to help you do your own work by talking a bit about what I think about this kind of prayer in general and about my own prayer in particular?

Yes, my friend, if this is what you want, I will gladly help you in any way I can. You are, after all, very important to me. I not only want to help you, I also want to share my life with you. At the same time, I have been doing a lot of work in my own prayer recently, and I

---

1. See my *To Love as God Loves: Conversations with the Early Church* (Minneapolis: Augsburg-Fortress, 1987).

have already been thinking a lot about prayer and the work of healing the wounds of the heart we all carry. My own stuff over the last year or two has included trying to learn to overcome my perfectionism and panic as I attempt to take up the flute again in my middle age; dealing with grief over the loss of my father; figuring out how to inhabit a human body; trying to overcome stubborn childhood shame and perfectionism; dealing with judgmentalism; and discovering gratitude and the mystery of grace, among other things.

I realize, of course, that our issues are not going to be the same. Still, my hope is that if I write you about some of this, you will find something here, perhaps indirectly as much as directly, that proves useful to you. Writing a few long letters about it all—short ones never work for me, which is why I am such an infrequent correspondent!—will help me, too, because it will give me a chance to clarify some of what I have been doing and mulling over lately.

I think it is so terribly important for Christians to overcome our reluctance to talk concretely and, most important, realistically about our experience of prayer. I realize that this is often not very easy. Growing up in my family, which in this respect was pretty typical if I can judge by what other people tell me of their families, we could talk about almost anything if we really had to, even about sex. Talk of prayer, however, was never suitable for "polite conversation," which, at home, meant any conversation at all. Prayer was regarded as too personal, too intimate, or maybe just too embarrassing. Certainly, to have enough interest in it even to bring it up was a mark of religious fanaticism.

Why do we have so much trouble around the topic of prayer even at church, I wonder? Partly, perhaps, we've been told all our lives that prayer is something we "ought to do" as Christians. We are not sure exactly how we are to go about doing it, but because we are supposed to know about it, we don't want to ask. Partly, perhaps, it is because we've been bullied or intimidated by people who have been happy to tell us not only that there is only one right way to pray, but that they will teach us how, whether we want to learn or not. Maybe we associate it in our minds with really holy people—or at least people pious enough that we don't feel comfortable around them.

Whatever the reason, however, it is too bad we feel like this. Prayer is such an ordinary, everyday, mundane thing. Certainly, people who pray are no more saints than the rest of us. Rather, they are people who want to share a life with God, to love and be loved, to speak and to listen, to work and to be at rest in the presence of God. Certainly, they are people who want the truth about themselves and about reality. They want to find the parts of themselves they would rather not acknowledge and bring them to God for love and healing. They want to learn how to be the loving, interiorly thriving people God created them to be. They aren't particularly holy, though. Mostly, they are just simply stubborn, persistent people who know that every close personal relationship of love, including ours with God, involves a lot of risk taking, a lot of being in the dark, and a lot of persistence through times of boredom.

On the other hand, the healing work of prayer is mundane all right, but it is still mightily mysterious. It has a long-term quality to it that both shapes and helps us understand the past and the future at the same time. I can give you an example of what I mean from something significant that came to me in my own prayer about a year ago at the end of a very long dry spell.

My troubles began when I finished my last writing project two years ago. Up till then it was the hardest thing I had ever written; the writing had both gone against my own academic training and run counter to my inhibitions against speaking to others of private family matters. As part of the work, I had also had to live all over again through some very painful childhood memories.

I had been worn out by it, and by the time I was finished I was ready to set aside that kind of project to work on something else I had looked forward to for a long time: writing a collection of stories about my mother's family in Kentucky that I intended to stand as a fitting witness to the braveries, the goodness, and the sufferings of the lives of these women and men who were my ancestors.

I was full of enthusiasm for the new project; I had the time, and I had the support of my dean at school. The only trouble was, as much as I wanted to, I found I couldn't write. Over the course of nearly a year I prayed about this problem daily, but nothing I had to say to God helped. Though I sat down faithfully at my computer every day, nothing much would come out of my brain. It was not as though I had a writer's block—I knew about those from experience. I didn't feel lazy or bored. It seemed, rather, that my mind had just been emptied of everything I wanted to say.

For a while, I accepted this as normal. After all, I had been writing steadily for a good long time without a break. Furthermore, it wasn't as though writing were the only thing I had been doing with myself in the past few years. I had been teaching and speaking and being a mother and a wife. On top of everything else, our daughter, Grace, was about to be married. I was tired; certainly, I needed a break. It seemed natural, therefore, that my mind should say to me, "I'm staying here; you go on ahead without me."

After recovering from the first shock of not being able to write, I accepted that I needed mental rest. Still, being compulsive in the ways I am around writing, I continued to sit at the computer every day for fear that the creative energies would start to flow and I wouldn't be there to take advantage of them.

Two months passed and it was time for Grace's wedding. Soon after, spring was over; summer came and receded into memory. School started up again in September, and still I was stumbling along on the computer as I had been in February. I began with good reason to worry seriously that I might never be able to write again. Throughout October I dragged myself drearily to and from my computer, and to and from my daily prayer, too. Nothing I said to God seemed to help. By the end of November, the panic I had eluded until now was squeezing me around the middle like the too tight waistband of an outgrown skirt.

Then one morning before class, as I was saying my prayers and worrying to God that I had somehow become a desert in which nothing would ever again grow, I found myself unexpectedly in the midst of a powerful image. In my mind I was standing in a fertile field covered with long, rippling late summer grass. In the field and to the left of my sight stood a wonderfully shaped apple tree whose boughs bent down under the weight of ripening red apples. At the back, through the white mist that hung over the whole scene I could faintly see a black, split-rail Kentucky fence enclosing the field and the apple tree.

Then, as I continued to look and to ponder what it was that I was seeing, the weather began to change. A strong wind blew in from the east, flattening the grass and swaying the boughs of the tree. The temperature dropped. In a moment hard sheets of icy rain were slanting across the field with great force, sending up sprays of mud as they rattled and hissed against the red earth out of which the grass grew. Silver puddles formed around the bases of the fence posts and in the bare spaces in the grass. As for me, I was drenched to the skin, bone-cold, and full of joy. Soon, the image faded, and I found myself back once again sitting on the green couch of my office. It was nearly time for class.

What did my prayer image mean to me then, and what does it mean to me now? First, there was the apple tree. What it stood for then and still stands for now is the lush, gnarled, spreading presence of God within me, mysteriously growing, full of nourishing apples that ripen in the cold rain, good and true and beautiful.

Then, there was the grassy field. From the moment I saw it, I understood that I was myself the field, and the grass that grew in it was the work I had to do that lay before me. What shape this work would take, I didn't know, and I didn't need to know, either. Rather, the whole image promised me that, in spite of appearances, I had not in fact become a desert. Things were growing within me lushly, even if I couldn't experience it happening in the present.

After that, there was the rain. The presence of this rain, heavy and cold as it was, told me that I was not yet where I would end up before the grass was ready to be mowed. The work in front of me was going to be hard. At the same time, I could expect that the coming rain, which would chill me to the bone, would *only* make me cold and uncomfortable. That which would make me grow would not do me harm. After all, it was the same God who was making the promises and calling me to this work from whom the rain would come.

Finally, there was the black fence bordering the back of the field, and here I have to confess to uncertainty. When I first saw the fence that day in my office, I wondered what on earth it was doing there. Then I heard these words spoken very clearly in my head: "It is for sitting and for climbing." But who is it, I asked myself, who is to do the sitting and climbing?

Though it was not at all clear to me at the time, it seems to me now that the fence in my image was meant to be a reminder that none of the most private, most internal work of prayer I or any of the rest of us do as Christians is ever "only for me" but is always as much for our brothers and sisters in Christ as it is for ourselves. All of us play and rest, too, on one another's prayers as much as we do on our own—that's what it means, after all to live in the communion of the saints.

At any rate, when I got up from my prayer that day in November, my writing problems had not gone away. What I did have, however, was a sure sense of confidence that things within me were growing. If I paid attention, held myself ready to go to work when the opportunity came, and was willing to be brave no matter how cold the rain might happen to be, the grass would grow and the apples would ripen until it was time to write again.

Sure enough, this is what happened. By Christmas I was back at it, doing work in my prayer and theological reflection that was as significant to me and certainly as hard as any I have yet done.

Until this time, much of my life since childhood had been lived in crisis. Over the last twelve or fifteen years, I had been able to find meaning and healing in it by understanding and living through these crises by way of crucifixion, death, and resurrection, the great festival of Easter. Now I was being called to the task of learning to live more of my life in the everyday world—metaphorically and liturgically speaking—in the Ordinary Time of the incarnation. Since you asked, this is the work about which I will write you.

Before I go on, however, to talk about the nitty-gritty of the prayer I've been facing lately, it seems to me that if I am to make the way I work clear to you in such a fashion that it really will be helpful to you, I will need to say something about the necessarily intertwined theological assumptions and the assumptions about prayer from which I now do this work.

I realize, of course, that though you are probably not one of them, for many people prayer and theology may not seem as though they have much to do with each other. One of the most important things I have learned over the years, however, is how fundamentally impossible it is at a practical level to separate prayer and theology. On the one hand, every bit of praying each of us ever does, whether in words, gestures, attitudes, or emotions, is always grounded in who we at least unconsciously think God is, what God is really like, and how we ourselves need to be in relation to God. Think of what you are saying about God and yourself, for example, if you feel the need to begin every prayer, not just public but private, too, with a confession of sin.

Equally, and on the other hand, every judgment we make about who God is and who we are with respect to God is directly going to encourage us to pray one way rather than another. Consider how we will have to present ourselves to God if we are convinced—as my classmates were when I was in seminary—that God's attention and love are focused not on the "petty concerns" of individuals, but rather only on the larger issues of social justice, like war and world hunger. Now consider what it means for our prayer if we truly believe, with the psalmist of Psalm 139, that God has not only known everything about us there is to know about us from before we were ever born, but that God takes a most intense personal interest in us, besides.

Theology and prayer are also linked in another subtle, but related way. Many folks think of "real" theology primarily as abstract and speculative talk about God and God's ways, and the more abstract and speculative and universal it is, the more serious it is. The fact is, nothing could be further from the truth. Like prayer, the work of real theology is saving work;[2] it is about learning to see God and understand reality and ourselves as we really are in order that we may grow and thrive and become the loving people God wants us to be. Prayer and theological reflection vitally need each other; they are two parts of a whole that cannot be separated.

But this is carrying us into my first theological assumption and assumption about prayer, which is this: Before anything else, above all else, beyond everything else, God loves us. God loves us extravagantly, ridiculously, without limit or condition. God is in love with us; God is besotted with us. God yearns for us.[3] God

---

2. A phrase used by my colleague Rebecca S. Chopp. See her *Saving Work: Feminist Practices of Theological Education* (Louisville: Westminster/John Knox, 1995).

3. This yearning language is characteristic language of Greek patristics, a wonderful gift of Christian platonism. See especially Dionysius the Psuedo-Areopagite in the "Divine Names," chapter 3.1, *Pseudo-Dionysius: The Complete Works*, trans. Colm Luibheid, Classics of Western Spirituality (New York: Paulist Press, 1987), p. 82.

does not love us "in spite of who we are" or "for whom God knows we can become." According to the wonderful fourth- and fifth-century teachers I have learned from and also teach myself, God loves us hopelessly as mothers love their babies,[4] and as tiny babies love everybody who smiles at them.[5] God loves us, the very people we are; and not only that, but, even against what we ourselves sometimes find plausible, God *likes* us.

Of course, we know that God loves us; we hear it all the time and we say it ourselves. Still, for a lot of us, saying it and believing it in our heads is one thing; knowing it to be true in our hearts, another. Certainly, of all the things I have come to believe about God over the years, nothing has been so hard for me to learn as this. Partly, this is because in the churches in which I grew up I was told that above all else God was good, and that God expected human beings to be good also. Because we—I—were not good, but sinners, I was actually deserving of the judgment of eternal condemnation and rejection. It was only because God loved me that I wasn't at that very moment in hell. All this seemed plausible enough to me; it fit exactly with the way I knew my very critical and demanding father saw me.

---

4. Macarian Homily 46.3. *Intoxicated by God: The Fifty Spiritual Homilies of Macarius,* trans. and introd. by George Maloney, S.J. (Denville, N.J.: Dimension Books, 1978).

5. Ephrem the Syrian, Hymn 13.12-15, in Hymns of the Nativity. *Ephrem the Syrian: Hymns,* trans. Kathleen McVey (New York: Paulist Press, 1989), p. 139.

He loved me, but it seemed to me that it was not for who I was; it was in spite of who I was.

The effect of this stuff on the way I related to God was perfectly predictable. I was terrified of God as a child; and though it took me a long time to admit it to myself, when I came to pray, I was still terrified of God as an adult. "Only trust God," I would hear people say. Trust God! I could hardly imagine sitting in God's presence as the person I actually was without feeling crushed with shame. Whatever I told myself I believed about God's loving me, what I really thought was that what God really liked doing was weighing up and judging every one of my faults, sins, flaws, and errors.

Only as an adult was I able at last to believe that God really isn't very interested in judging everything I do, and that God truly does love the very person I am, as God loves all people. How that happened I've told elsewhere.[6] What I need to say here, however, is this: I believe we do awful damage to ourselves when we tell ourselves and others that God loves us in spite of who we are, and then on top of everything else, exhort ourselves to love God in return. As a child, I used to feel such fear and despair that I couldn't "have faith" and love God no matter how hard I tried. Now, I often think, gratefully, that the very fact that I couldn't was a gift of

---

6. See *Memories of God: Theological Reflections on a Life* (Nashville: Abingdon Press, 1995), chapter 1, where I wrote about this long process.

God's grace. What would it have done to me if I had managed to love the very God I believed found everything about me contemptible? What does it do to any of us? If nothing else, the use of such "in spite of" language of judgment keeps us from being able to be truthful with ourselves in God's presence. Certainly, it prevents us thriving and enjoying the presence of God as God meant us to do.

The first assumption that I make, therefore, is that God loves me as God loves all people, without qualification. The second is related to it, and it was also a long time coming to me. According to such great early Christian teachers of the first five centuries whom I teach, such as Irenaeus, Athanasius, Anthony, and Gregory of Nyssa, all human beings are created in the image of God. To them, to be in the image of God means that all of us are made for the purpose of knowing and loving God and one another and of being loved in turn, not literally in the same way God knows and loves, but in a way appropriate to human beings.

They also teach, however, that we live in a fallen world, that is, in a world in which the image of God within all of us is not lost but rather damaged. Because of this damage we have a very hard time actually knowing and loving either God or other people. This is because we are too blinded by our own wounds, which they usually call "the passions," to even see the noses on our own faces much less anybody else.[7] Among these wounds are our fears and anxieties about the past and the future, our destructive anger or inability to be appropriately angry when we need to be, our envy, our poisonous shame, our bitter regret over what might have been, our numbness that we cultivate to dull the pain, and so forth.

It is important to pay attention to the language I am using here. Along with my teachers from the early church, I am describing what is wrong with our individual lives not so much in terms of *sin that needs to be repented of*, as in terms of *injuries to our ability to love and be loved that need to be healed*.[8]

This is not because I don't believe in the existence of sin and repentance, because I do. Though I realize that the line between "deliberate" and "inadvertent" is often very vague, I still find it helpful to speak of sin in situations where we make real, even if half unconscious, choices in situations when we know better and are able

---

7. These writers were not using the term "passion" as we frequently use it today, that is, as a synonym for strong emotion. For the early church's understanding of the passions and how they affect us in our own lives see my *To Love as God Loves: Conversations with the Early Church*, chapter 4.

8. Anthony, who was revered in a special way in the ancient world as a founder of monasticism, speaks in one of his letters of "the great wound" afflicting humankind. *The Letters of Saint Antony the Great*, trans. Derwas Chitty (Fairacres, Oxford: SLG Press, 1980), Letter III, p. 9.

to do better than we do. Sin makes us close our eyes deliberately to others' needs and desires. Roughly speaking, sin results in our hurting ourselves and other people, sometimes fatally, because it suits us or because we can't be bothered to do otherwise. For sin we need repentance.

There is, however, at least one serious difficulty with the way we modern Christian folk want to use sin and repentance language to cover all or most of the causes of our individual unhappiness. It is that it seems to suggest to us that everything wrong in our lives is somehow our own fault, even if we can't see how that can be the case. This leads some of us to be demoralized in such a way that we just give up and feel that everything we do is wrong. For others of us it has the opposite effect; it being obvious that we can't individually be responsible for everything wrong with life, we end up refusing to accept responsibility for the things we actually are responsible for. In both cases, whether from fear and inadequacy or from irrelevance, prayer becomes hard for us, and life does, too.

The fact is that both our own common sense and our teachers from the early church tell us that most of our serious difficulties are far more complex in origin than we would like to think. A large number of things that cause us to hurt ourselves and others come from hurtful ways of being and relating that we learned in our larger culture and in our families to think of as good and right.

One obvious example of something hurtful that we learn in our culture is the idea that real men should be stoic and not take feelings seriously, theirs or anybody else's. Some of what continues to hurt us and makes us hurt others dates back to particular things that happened to us in childhood or babyhood. Some of it has as much to do with the temperament we were born with as with anything else.

Telling myself that my depression or irritability or perfectionism or fear of loss is sinful and an offense against God for which I must repent does not help me deal with them, and it certainly does not help me pray. Rather, such self-judgment tends only to undercut me and drive me away from God. It increases my sense of helpless guilt one more time when I discover that, as one of the early monastic teachers used to say, "violence will not drive out violence."[9] Though I, or any of us, may learn to control our behavior, it is very rare that we can simply get tough with ourselves, repent, and stop being the way we are. On the other hand, acknowledging depression, perfectionism, and fear of loss to be the wounds that they are gives us the wide space and the long time we need to do the work of healing and to live in the expectation of God's grace. Abba Poemen,

---

9. Part 5, "Of Lust," 27 in "The Sayings of the Fathers," in *Western Asceticism*, Selected Translations with Introductions and Notes by Owen Chadwick, Library of Christian Classics (Philadelphia: Westminster Press, 1958), p. 68.

a teacher of the ancient Egyptian desert, used to say that it is "not knowing what happened that prevents us from going on to something better."[10] Recognizing our wounds for what they are, namely wounds in the image of God that keep us from loving what God wants healed, keeps us from being paralyzed by shame and guilt. It energizes us to do in our prayer the painful work of introspection and memory that it takes to seek the healing of these sometimes excruciating injuries.

This brings us to my next assumption, which is that a good portion of the long-term work of our personal prayer is and ought to be seeking healing for the damaged image of God within us. Not everyone agrees with this. There are many people within the Christian tradition, especially from the period of the Reformation to the present, who don't like this way of talking because, they say, it is too psychological, too self-centered, and too focused on human beings instead of God. Prayer, they believe, should be directed away from ourselves. It should primarily consist in the worship of God and should be done for the glory of God.

I have already said that the majority of the teachers of the fourth, fifth, and sixth centuries within the tradi-

---

10. Poemen 200, *The Sayings of the Desert Fathers: The Alphabetical Collection,* trans. Benedicta Ward (London and Oxford: Mowbray, 1977), p. 194.

tion of early monasticism I have found so particularly helpful for myself point out, however, that because we are all so wounded by anger, fear of the future, envy, depression, and so forth, there *is* no way that we really can know and love *God* until we begin to be able to know *ourselves* and the people around us as we and they really are. To do this kind of knowing, however, we first need some healing.

How can we celebrate God's forgiving nature if we aren't able to give or receive forgiveness ourselves? How can we truly express gratitude to God for God's gifts if we are so beaten down by the things that have happened to us that we aren't even aware of those gifts? How can we worship God as just if we haven't sorted out our own confusion between *God* the father with our own *human* father who was manifestly arbitrary in his dealings with his children? These teachers tell us, and I have experienced for myself, that if we ever are going to love and truly worship the actual God who made and loves us, then the prayer of most of us at least a significant part of the time needs to aim at working toward just this sort of healing so that we can see and know and share a life with God.

"Wounds!" I can hear you, a little disturbed, interrupting me at last. "You've been through all these theological presuppositions, and I simply don't think you are really taking sin seriously. How can you spend so much time describing what is clearly sin in terms of wounds? What do you have to say about how much God hates sin?" I can only ask you in return, my friend, why are we Christians so convinced that when God looks at us what God sees before anything else is our sin?

How well I remember the first time the alternative to that really sunk in for me. I was reading a book by a British theologian named Margaret Hebblethwaite, who was simultaneously trying to rear three little children under the age of six, and pray and reflect theologically on her experience.[11] The book was her own attempt to think about who God was from the perspective of her trials and pleasures as a mother. Needless to say, since she was an honest woman, a lot of what she wrote was just plain painful to read, but there was one passage that particularly struck me. She was considering the possibility that God as our mother loves us with exactly the same delight as mothers love their little children. It was easy enough from that point for me to remember looking at my own refrigerator door upon which my two-year-old daughter's paintings had once hung. I recalled very well what the pictures looked like, drips and all. How irrelevant those drips were to me! Instead, I was filled up to the top with pride and happiness and

11. *Motherhood and God* (London: Geoffrey Chapman, 1984), p. 15. I want to be careful to distinguish her reflections here from my own. I do not know, in fact, if she would agree with me that God's interest in our sins is minimal compared to God's delight in us.

pleasure in my child. "My daughter!" I had thought. "What an artist!"

Now we get to the important part of what was suggested to me. While I remembered looking at Grace's pictures and feeling this pride and love, it occurred to me to wonder, What if, when God looks at God's children and what we do, God is struck first, not by all the awful things we do, but by God's love for us? What if God sees very well the terrible, hateful messes we make, but says instead, "Yes, I see it all, but how much more important it is that they are so dear to me. The baby paintings they make are beautiful to me, and I love them so very much I can hardly bear the pain of it."

My friend, how is an exclusive language of sin helpful if it keeps us from feeling safe and loved in God's presence, and indeed, drives us away? Surely, if God loves us with the same tenderness I felt for my own babies, how can God help seeing us like this? And once we believe that God does see us like this, how can we help wanting to learn to set aside our sense of our own unworthiness in the presence of God so that we can love God in return?

All of this brings me right up to my next theological assumption, which is this: As we have just seen, in moving toward, living into, and trying to understand our relationship with God, anthropomorphic language, images, and experiences are not just helpful; they are also fully appropriate.

I know this may seem to you a difficult and surprising statement. After all, I know that you have experienced anthropomorphic language and images of God in ways that have been horribly oppressive to you. Not just you, but many other people of my acquaintance, men and women both, spend their whole lives trying to escape from childhood images of God as a stern old man with a long white beard sitting on a throne. As for myself, you know already how, for many years, I struggled with deep wounds caused by my inability to understand what it could mean for me as a woman to be made in the image of God, if all the images of God I had were male and I were female.

One way we've tried in the past to escape from this problem caused by dangerous human images of God is simply to decide that all human images are inappropriate as they are applied to God. After all, we used to say in seminary as we wrestled with all this, we know that God's ways are not our ways nor God's thoughts our thoughts. God is a spirit; God really isn't like us. Certainly, this means that no human images or names can really be appropriately applied to God in any but the most loosely metaphorical manner.

Of course, in some significant senses we were and are not only right when we say this; a large amount of the energy of the early church was devoted to arguing just this point about the transcendence of God.[12] Whatever else we might want to claim about God, we cannot get away from the fact that God is not in our control to manipulate as we see fit, no matter how good our reasons or purposes. God is not simply like a very admirable human being, only bigger. God does not have a human body or a human personality in the same way we do. In some significant ways, God is not predictable to us, nor can we know God in the same way we think we can know a human being.

The trouble is, neither in the long nor in the short run is this satisfying. We have been made in such a way that to be human is to be in relationship with others. This is so true in fact, that it is probably no exaggeration to say that we cannot even learn how to become human beings or grow as human beings without participating in relationships. It is natural, therefore, for us to yearn for intimacy with God, for closeness, for participation in relationships with God.

Fortunately, or rather, blessedly, scripture and the tradition both are very clear in insisting that God can and does relate to us in the most intimate of ways. Jesus tells us that God's interest in us is so personal and specific to us that God knows how many hairs we have

---

12. It was in the controversy with the Arians that the significance of all this became clear in the early church.

on our heads, and neither scripture nor the teachers of the early church are the least bit embarrassed to describe our relationship with God in human terms. God can be with us as a mother with her finger-painting baby, or a passionate lover, a tender father, a friend, a spouse, or even as a helpless and trusting baby; and in each case, something is called forth from us that not only relates us to God, it also makes us more ourselves as human beings.

But how can we still use this intimate language of human relationship once we have accepted that all language about God is metaphorical? There are two parts to the answer. One lies in the meaning of the incarnation and the other in what it means to be made in the image of God.

First, the incarnation. No matter how many different approaches to God we find in Christian history, the tradition itself has been unanimous in affirming that, when God really wanted to reveal God's self to us in the plainest and truest possible way, God did not do this by coming among us as a disembodied principle or "pure" spirit. God came among us as an actual human being. God was born into a human family in the person of Jesus. Jesus lived a human life like the rest of us, died, was buried and resurrected, and all the time he was surrounded by human beings, his mother, his friends, his disciples, and many other people, too, to whom he was intimately and personally related.

You, of course, might still say, yes, but all of that relating to the people around him we see Jesus doing in scripture only demonstrates he was a human being; it says nothing about what God is like or how God who is a spirit really acts. The gospel of John has an answer for this. When Philip in anguish asks Jesus to *show* him the father to whom Jesus claims to be going, Jesus says to him, "I can't understand it. After all this time how can you still not understand? Don't you know that the one who has seen me *has seen* the father?"

As Christians we claim that Jesus was a human being who was not only made in the image of God. He is the one whose humanity has shown us what the un-wounded image of God is supposed to look like. Whenever we are tempted to give in to the voices even within the Christian tradition itself that suggest to us that "real" truth must be expressed only in terms that are universal and impersonal, free of emotion, free of the messy particularities of our ordinary lives, and free of relationships, God comes to us in the form of the incarnation to say no.

The fact is, if we know that being in the image of God means being able to love fully and to allow ourselves to be loved, then we cannot help understanding that real love is always incarnate, always particular. Not even Jesus loved in some abstract, pure spiritual realm; he loved real people.

As for us human beings, it seems clear to me that the only thing making our messy and particular individual loves possible is the image of God functioning within us. This is another reason, besides the fact of the incarnation, that we never need to be apologetic about seeking to relate to God as we would to the human beings we love, whether to God as lover, friend, or parent: all human relationships of love are what they are only because they are modeled already on who the God in whose image we are made actually already is.

"Oh no," I can hear you worrying some more. "Does this mean that you believe that there are no serious problems with trying to relate to God in terms of human relationships?" Of course I don't think that. This is why we must pay attention at all sorts of levels at once. At one level of grace, if we find that trying to relate to God as mother, say, or spouse, seems to be sucking the life out of us instead of giving us life, we are being given a clue about the nature of our own wounds. We are learning where we need to work in our prayer. At the same time, we are being called to discover whether there is something in the way in which we are conceiving of the relationship that we are entering into with God that is destructive of human life and therefore false to who God is.

If, for example, we try to relate to God as mother and we assume that as a mother God wants us to be helpless babies who never talk, we are sure to have trouble. In this case, we need to think through both our experiences of being mothered and mothering and our theology, which has been supported and made sense of them.

Concretely put, this means that if we are having difficulty with a particular image such as "mother," we also have to look and see if there is something in the image of motherhood through which we are approaching God that intersects with our own experience that is poisoning both the image through which we are trying to relate to God, and the primary similar human relationship. If this is the case, then we need to seek healing in our prayer for the wounds around our original human relationships that are now causing us trouble.

This gets me to the last—and shortest, though not least significant—theological assumption I want to state for you in this letter. It is this. In spite of the real truth to be found in the so-called "Protestant principle" that salvation is by faith alone, for the early church folk I work on, human salvation, if it is understood as something more than simply getting to heaven, is never *only* the result either of God's grace, any more than it is *only* the result of our own hard work. This is my experience as well.

It is true that without grace, without God's active presence, we would have no hope for healing these terrible wounds of the heart we carry. The fact is, however, that God very rarely comes into our lives and hits us over the head with help in such a way that we can't resist it. Rather, God has made us in the image of God for friendship with Godself. Though God will often intervene to help when we can't figure out how to help ourselves, God doesn't generally run over us disrespectfully or patronizingly to fix us up without our own active participation.

This means that, while we are dependent absolutely on God for our healing, the work we do in prayer really makes a difference. God provides the grace and the healing. Our job is to pray for the graceful presence of the God we need, to seek it, to make ourselves available to it, to wrestle with it, to endure boredom for the sake of it, to be wounded by it, to let ourselves be surprised by it, to let it show us things in ourselves we don't want to see, to let it bring up painful memories, to deliberately expose ourselves to it, to be humbled by it, to be fed by it, to laugh with it, and above all to ask for it and expect to receive it. It is tough, I know, but it is worth it.

All this being true, I want to say one more thing before I close. In your letter you mentioned to me that one of the wounds you are wrestling with is your memory of your father in your growing up years. As a result, you say, you can hardly stand even to try to pray to God as father. Please, please, don't give up. Take advantage of this way of praying. However powerful your father is, after all, he is not God. God as father is not destructive of you or controlling as your father has been. Still, I'm not sure that you, or any of us, can ever know that what I say is true without first going ahead and learning to relate to God as father face to face in our prayer. I know it's painful, but it is worth it to get to the other side of it, and let your father just be your father and God, God.

Know that you are, as always, in my heart. Until next time,

*Roberta*

# The Healing Work of Prayer

*My dear friend,*

It was a great relief to get your letter. As you can imagine, I've been more than eager to hear how you were faring as you tried to sort through all I had sent in my own letter to you. I'm glad you say you found a lot to think about in it, some of it even helpful!

Also, don't think I didn't notice and appreciate what I'm sure you thought of as the kind and discreet way you told me you weren't entirely satisfied with my letter. I do know that you had actually hoped for some concrete, practical advice on how to go about doing the healing kind of prayer. You didn't really think I would just give you some sort of prayer list to check off, did you? Try to be patient with me, if you can. I really meant it when I said that I couldn't even begin to answer your request without first telling you about the intertwined theological assumptions and assumptions about prayer I have to work from. I do believe, after all, that you will need to keep pondering those very assumptions as you do your own work. I know I certainly do.

Now that we've gotten all that out of the way (and I do hope you aren't too out of sorts from my crotchetiness) I'm ready to go ahead and start in on what you've asked.

Let me begin by repeating what I said at the end of my last letter: for the healing of the image of God in us so that we may know and love others and allow ourselves to be known and loved as God intends, both our own very hard work and God's grace are equally necessary. Experience teaches that neither can we heal ourselves by willpower alone, nor will God come and heal us without our active cooperation.[1]

As for God's part in our prayer, I will come back to it at the end of this letter. Before I get to there, however, I would like to point to some necessary practical preliminaries about what it takes to go about the healing work of prayer from our human end.

The first is one of those things that seems obvious to me, but which you tell me has always caused you trouble. However much you would like me to, I really

---

1. The early church teachers called this combination of human and divine effort "synergism," which means "working-with-ism."

can't tell you just what to do in your prayer, and neither can anybody else. It doesn't matter how many books on prayer you will ever read; there simply is no one right way to pray. We are different from each other, and our prayer is necessarily going to be as varied as we are. Because we—not just you and I, but all of us—are different in our life-experiences, our working theologies, our temperaments, our physical conditions, our limitations, and perhaps most especially in the way God works within us, your prayer is going to have to be very different from mine.

Furthermore, your own prayer isn't even going to be the same all year round. As for myself, my prayer with school going on now in October is very different from my prayer not three months ago in July. This means that one of the main tasks of your prayer is to find what suits you, personally. I realize, of course, that coming as you do from a tradition that is very specific about there being only one right way to pray, learning to trust yourself may prove to be very hard.

Now for my second preliminary. Again, I know that once you start in on something, you want to keep at it till you've seen it through to the end. My friend, I think you are going to have to give this up. Believe me when I say that none of us can wrestle all the time in our prayer with the things that really hurt us and have been hurting us for a long time. For me, at least, this high-energy, often painful work has to be intermittent. Depending on the intractability of what I am looking at, I may spend six weeks on a specific problem, or three days. I may go all the way through a problem to its end, or I may work for a short time, leave it alone for a few weeks or months, and then come back to it when it presses on me. Going about it in this intermittent way, sometimes it takes years before I know I'm finished with something in my prayer. In any case, you need to be aware that this work is not steady. Often I go months at a time without doing this kind of praying, and this makes it infinitely easier and less all-consuming.

You will see why this is important when I remind you of what by now you can't fail to know—that this kind of praying is nearly always painful and often excruciating. Not that I think pain is worth anything at all for its own sake, you understand. Still, as we face what is hurting us by digging up, reliving, and thinking through old memories, pain is inevitable, and the only way we can be willing to tolerate it now is because we know that we are trying to escape it on a more permanent basis. It always helps me to remember that I can't avoid pain by refusing to do this work, since it is my ongoing hurting that is driving me toward it in the first place.

The third thing I have to say at the outset about this kind of prayer is that it is also risky. I remember a conversation I had with one of my brothers a few years ago. He had been unhappy with some things about his job and someone had told him if he "turned it all over to the Lord" he would find peace. When he asked me if I thought it was true, I could only laugh. Even everyday prayer depends on our willingness to find out things about ourselves and our lives that we may not want to know. Sometimes it puts us in a position where we have to make decisions we don't want to make. Especially at the beginning, and especially if our experience of God has been difficult, it can also depend on our willingness to make ourselves vulnerable with God in very scary ways.

Fourth, if we are going to do this kind of praying, we have to be willing to be stubborn and persistent with God. We have to decide when we go into a project that, though we may go away from it for a while, when it comes to seeking healing of the image of God within us, we are not going to give up. In fact, we will have to be exactly like the widow with the unjust judge, and Jacob wrestling the angel for a blessing. We've got to be willing to work slowly and take twenty years if we have to, but we are not going to go away until God gives us what we need.

Don't worry, friend, I can hear you asking even at this distance, "But isn't being stubborn the exact opposite of having faith? Isn't it arrogant?" I answer, no, not as I see it. Having faith doesn't mean just sitting there, trusting that if you are quiet and don't get in the way God will look after you. It doesn't mean believing everything you are told without doubts, either. Remember the father of the sick boy whom Jesus asked, "Do you believe I can heal your son?" "Yes," he said, "I believe; help my unbelief!"

What having faith does mean is saying to God, "It was you in Jesus who taught me to pray to you, 'Give us this day our daily bread.' I am not asking you for a bicycle for my own fun and pleasure. I am holding you to your promise to give me the basic things I need in order to be the person you created me to be. I'm asking for your help, and I am doing my own part in this work just as faithfully as I know how. As Jesus taught me, I will continue persistently, doggedly, and stubbornly to wrestle with all of this and you until you give me what I need and bless me." Is this arrogant? If it is, I believe it is God who teaches us to be that way.

My friend, I have to talk with you about one more thing before we go on to the concrete details of how I do the hard work of prayer you're asking about. For most of us, if we are ever going to have the courage and stubbornness to face and wrestle with the things that hurt us, and take the risks we'll have to take to do it, we have to know that we have a safe and dependable space in which to do our wrestling and risk taking. This is why I think that all of us, you included, need to make a commitment to a practice of daily prayer. It is our knowledge, no matter how dim, of God's gentle trust-worthiness that will carry us through the hard parts of our work, but none of us can find out apart from experience that God will be trustworthy when we need God to be.

What our presence with God should be like in this regular daily prayer I'm talking about here is something I'd like to think about with you next. I know that, like many of the rest of us, you have had laid on you some pretty unreasonable expectations about prayer. You said in your last letter, for example, that you had always been told that when you pray, you need to be fully present to God, alert and in a worthy frame of mind, "sincere" and full of trust and love, or you haven't truly prayed. This unrealistic demand has been the undoing of more people than you. However other people may tell you they pray, I don't believe there is anyone anywhere who prays like this all the time or even most of the time, and I will tell you why in a little while. For now, let me suggest that you throw away your unrealistic expectations and replace them with a new conviction: that your ordinary prayer must have as its foundation a commitment just simply to show up for it every day in whatever condition you are in.

My friend, I am aware that you are often seduced by images of the nobleness of prayer. I also know that the reasons I've already given for a practice of daily prayer are not particularly noble, nor is the language of "showing up" very noble, either. This is because I find high-flown language and ideas to be disastrous when they are applied to prayer. Actual prayer isn't noble most of the time, any more than any of our other actual relationships, if they are based in being with another real person rather than being based in our false fantasies about ourselves and the other person.

Everyday prayer in ordinary time is just not very inspiring to look at from the outside most of the time, and we will only demoralize ourselves if we think it should be otherwise. The fact is, we often are going to go for long stretches where we can barely do more than sit in God's presence with our minds wandering. Sometimes we fall asleep; sometimes we feel resentful or half dead. There can be all sorts of good, practical reasons this is so. In some cases it is because we are so unavoidably busy or tired that we hardly know what we are doing. In other cases, it is because we are still learning that God is somebody we want to be with. We may be angry at God and unable even to recognize it yet, or our mistaken notion that God wants us only when we are "good" is getting in our way. Sometimes, it is because we are human beings, and that is just the way prayer is some of the time for human beings.

What is important, though, is that however we are, in whatever frame of mind we are, we do simply show up. When I first started teaching in seminary, I used to get so tired at school that I could barely make it home, and on many a night in September, to my shame, I would fall asleep at the dinner table while the children and my husband were talking to me. One of my fantasies in those days was that I would take a sandwich to school for supper and come home more alert and rested after dinner so that I could be present to them in the way they really needed. The fact was, however, I knew this was all a fantasy. I was a member of a family; whatever condition I was in, it was obvious to me that I belonged with my family at dinnertime. It is the same with God (see the fourth theological assumption in my previous letter!). God wants us to show up for our prayer, and not some idealized version of ourselves, either. God is the one who made us; God knows very well what our human limitations are. As I said in the very first theological assumption, God not only loves us; it is the very people we are that God wants.

How do I visualize a regular practice of "just showing up"? For some people some of the time, it may be rather formal: scripture reading, meditation, and conversation with God. For others, the whole of our prayer may consist of what is sometimes called "centering prayer." For others still, it may involve sitting quietly in the presence of God receiving whatever comes in the way of images or thought or nothing at all; for others, there will be a strong physical element like running or walking. You must experiment to find what is right for you.

The important thing is that you make it easy on yourself to establish this habit. This means finding a place that works for you and gives you quiet for a little while. It can be a walk-in closet, a living room, or a desk in the library; what matters is that it suits you. Then, pick a time of day, morning, afternoon, or evening, that actually is practical for you. You need to be especially careful when you decide on a length of time to be practical. For some folks, this may be a half-hour or more; for others, even ten minutes may seem long. This is not the occasion to decide what you "ought" to do; there is no "ought to" about this. Remind yourself instead, over and over, that what other people do or say you should do is irrelevant; what you want (not ought) to do is whatever it takes to make it possible for you to spend a little time every day in God's presence.

There are some people, however, who still will find this hard to do. If you are one, let me ask you, my friend, to please be as easy on yourself as you can bring yourself to be. I have found over the years that when people have this kind of difficulty, which is of a different sort from the everyday problem of not being able to be fully present all the time in prayer, there is a good reason for it that needs to be respected, even if they don't know what that reason is. It may be that at some time in your life the God you have encountered is simply too scary for you to feel safe with in prayer. You may be associating God with one or both of your parents in a way that is destructive of you. It might be that your own sense of unworthiness, or your sense of "oughtness" makes prayer difficult for you. It could even be that in the past you have been given such rigid models of prayer that your whole being rebels against any structure at all. Remember, we are talking about wounds here, not sin. Even if it should be that your problem is partly your own fault, you need to treat yourself with the same gentleness you would treat anyone else.

In any case, if you are one of these persons, I suggest that you try picking a book you *enjoy* reading—I like detective novels, myself—or some music you *enjoy* listening to, or perhaps a crossword puzzle or some handwork you like to do. Then, sit down and tell God that you would like to spend in God's presence whatever time you have decided to give to your prayer. Make yourself as comfortable as you can, then do what you have chosen to do knowing that you are doing it in God's presence. At the end of your time, say good-bye to God, get up, and go about your business.

Is this prayer? Is the time you spend reading or listening to music in the presence of the people you love real time together? Of course it is. Prayer is not just talking to God any more than friendship and marriage are just conversation. Prayer is sharing ordinary life, with its ordinary silences, distractions, pains, and pleasures, with God. After a while, if you are able to do what you enjoy in God's presence, you will begin to trust God just a little bit. When the time comes to find other ways to pray, you will know it and do it, and God will help you, too.

Having said all that about the importance of ordinary, everyday prayer and the need for "just showing up," I feel a little more ready to suggest to you, as you asked in your letter, how you yourself might go about doing the kind of work of prayer on some of the really hard issues that have made you unhappy, unable to love fully, and unable to know yourself to be loved.

If you decide to try to work in this way yourself, let me urge you again to remember every minute that I am not suggesting a rigid method, a list of steps to follow. There is no right way or wrong way about this kind of prayer. I am merely telling you what I have worked out over the years for myself. Please take what you find that is helpful to you, then, and use it or modify it in a way that suits you, and discard the rest.

First, let me suggest that you wait to begin your work until a particular problem that has really caused you difficulty for a long time (something like your own perfectionism, for example, or your insecurity about the future) presses in on you in such a way that you can't get away from it. There are two reasons for waiting until it really hurts. On the one hand, you will have more access to your pain than usual, which means you will also have more access to the reasons for your pain. On the other hand, God will have more access to you. At the same time, since you will already be hurting anyway, you won't be so tempted to quit by thinking you can avoid pain by refusing to face the problem head on.

Once you have decided to begin this work, next try to narrow down what you are dealing with as far as possible so that you can actually address it directly in your prayer. If what you are feeling is something like "no matter what I do, I can never do anything right," the process of narrowing down may feel very difficult. After all, you are making a judgment about your experience of your whole life! Nevertheless, this narrowing-down process is a crucial part of the work you will need to do. The fact is, you almost certainly never do everything badly; if you are going to do anything about it, you are going to need to know exactly in what circumstances you feel this way and in which circumstances you don't. I suggest you ask God in your prayer to help you figure this out.

Suppose you discover that you particularly feel this way in groups of people. One thing to do next is to try to recall the very first time you felt that way as a child. Notice that I didn't say, try to recall what you would think of as the first analogous situation when you were a child and then think about it. This is important. More often than not this will not work if you start with this kind of intellectual analysis. At the beginning, you've got to go for the feelings.

Let's say you have just been demoralized trying to speak about something you value to a group of people at church. You might expect, for example, that it would be helpful to jump directly to the memory of an event in childhood where the same kind of event occurred. For myself, I frequently find that there are two problems with such a jump.

First, even if I later discover that my mental connection of the two events was a true one, usually, beginning with the intellectual connection doesn't get me back into the memory in a way that helps me relive it and so work with it. Only approaching it through the pathway of the memory of a similar *feeling* allows me to do that.

Second, it is almost always the case that when I have not been able to get internal access to what is hurting me in such a way that I can actually address it in my prayer, it is because I have been mistaken in my analysis of what it was that had been hurting me in the first place. In other words, I had been connecting up the wrong things in my head, and then trying to see what these slightly wrong connections meant. Of course this effort was bound to end in failure, because I had made wrong connections to begin with. To put all this in other terms, it is often the case that I am unable to see where the actual analogies are between my adult life and my childhood until I am clear about what the content of the feelings, present and ancient, actually is.

Because it is so important to me that you understand this, let me give you a rather lengthy example of what I mean. After having had my feelings hurt by my mother right before Lent several years ago and having unfairly snapped at her for it, I decided I had to work on my own touchiness, which was hurting me and the other people I loved as well. This did not seem to me to be too hard a project for my prayer, because I imagined it would take no effort at all to connect my adult touchiness with my parents' childhood criticism of me. After several days of working fruitlessly on all this in my prayer, however, it became obvious to me that I was trying to work in the wrong place.

I knew, therefore, that it was time to go back and pay closer attention to what it was precisely that I had actually been feeling in the present when I believed my mother was criticizing me, so that I could recall just when it actually was that I had felt that very particular way in the past. Surprisingly, after a certain amount of digging, I was able to recall clearly feeling that same way, not in an incident at home, but rather when I was cruelly teased in elementary school by some boys in my class. At last, I had found the emotional connection that would allow the intellectual work of analysis, and the healing work of God, to begin touching where it really hurt.

At any rate, to get back to looking at the whole process of recovering memories in prayer, let's assume that, after a certain amount of work, you have managed to get hold of a particular memory of a feeling. It is very likely that you will not have much more than the feeling itself and one or two other very hazy details. Now it is time to attempt to pull up the rest of the memory into consciousness. Usually what makes this easier for me is to work at recalling other physical details of what I am trying to remember: what the room smelled like; what the light looked like; the textures of surfaces within my reach; what I was wearing; whether I was sleepy; who else was there; where I was sitting, standing, or lying with respect to the other people or objects in my memory; and so forth.

The point here is not to remember everything in photographic detail. It is to get far enough into the memory that you can walk around in it and experience it with the double perspective of the child you were and the adult you are now. Then you will have a place in the painful past to stand as you try to understand what the child you were thought happened, and what conclusions that child drew from what she or he thought about the world and the child and God, about what was good and bad, safe and dangerous for life.

If you find, however, that you really can't retrieve much else, then there are several things you might try to move further along. For myself, this is the point at which I will close my eyes and ask God to send me another memory. What this memory will be like when it comes can vary a lot. Sometimes what I remember will be something I've never really forgotten, but I haven't thought of it before in this context. At other times, it will be entirely new, and sharp and clear like the images in a dream. Yet again, it may be hazy, a detail of an event that I need to sit patiently with and tease out.

Sometimes no memory will ever come while I am awake, but in the next few days I will dream about whatever it is I am trying to retrieve. Have I mentioned how important I think dreams can be to our prayer? I think most of us need to learn to pay more attention to them than we often do. Paul says that the Holy Spirit searches our depths, and I believe it. A dream can be an invaluable gift God dredges up out of our depths that we otherwise may not have access to.

On a surprising number of occasions when I was confused about what I actually was feeling or thinking, for example, I have dreamed something that gave me a vital clue that helped me work it out. This was certainly the case of one dream I had in which Richard, my husband, was murdered in my great-aunt Blacky's green-tiled bathroom.[2] The dream came in response to my asking God for help in understanding the purpose of the crucifixion. What I got was terrible and bloody, and it showed me exactly what I understood in my heart that the crucifixion was about. Not all dreams are so painful as that one, of course. In fact, for me frequently they can be just the opposite as they direct me away from what I have experienced as a stony past into a

2. See *Memories of God*, chapter 4, for this dream and what followed from it.

living and life-giving future. I had some wonderful dreams when I first fell in love with Richard.

At any rate, let's assume that, however you've gotten it, you have become connected with an event of your childhood through that memory of a feeling, and you have reclaimed enough of that memory that you can start thinking it through profitably. Now it is time to start work with your memory to seek healing.

The first thing you will need to do is to ask yourself what you, *as a child*, thought actually was happening that formed the content of that formative memory. Suppose, for example, that you are recalling a period when neither of your parents paid any attention to you, and you felt lost, bewildered, and shamed by their lack of attention. How did you interpret their behavior when you were the child in the memory? Perhaps you can recall thinking that they didn't want you anymore, or that they had stopped loving you for some reason you couldn't understand. Perhaps you decided that you had caused their behavior by being bad.

Then, once you have figured out as best you can what the child you were thought was the reason for what happened, it is time to look again at the present and ask yourself if you have unconsciously continued as an adult to accept the child's judgments. Have you, for example, continued to believe in your heart that your parents were not available to you then because you were bad?

Or that they no longer love you, still? What consequences in the present have come with your ancient
explanations? In my experience, what you discover may
very well explain why you still cannot bring yourself to
go against your parents' expectations: improbable as it
may appear to be, you are helplessly afraid they will
leave you again as they left you before.

Now, suppose you have discovered as much as you
have been able about your ancient assumptions and
how they have carried into the present. Now you are in
a position to begin, to use Abba Poemen's phrase, to "go
on to something better." Start by asking yourself honestly whether the child's explanations for what happened really were the right ones. Do you know
something as an adult that the child either didn't know,
or knew but wasn't able, as a child, to value as an adult
would? Do you know of tensions between your parents
that would have made them unavailable to you at that
time? Was one of them out of work? Was another child
born about then? An in-law present in the household
and creating stress? A move? Do you have reason to
think your parents lied to you at the time about what
was happening and you believed them and have continued to half believe them in the present? Perhaps they
were letting you take the blame for something that you
can see now was not your fault. A close friend of mine,
for example, was told by her mother that her father
would not stop drinking unless she was a good girl; he

did stop, but her fear of the consequences of being "bad" has haunted her life ever since.

At this point, as you find yourself getting some clarity about what you are examining, it is time to begin looking at some crucial questions about the way your childhood interpretation of what happened in the event you are remembering has intersected with and formed your childhood—and adult—theology. Since as children we carry over what we know about our parents and apply it to God, what conclusions from your childhood experience did you draw about who God is and what God's expectations about you are? Did you decide that, if your own parents abandoned you emotionally because you were "bad," if you didn't watch out, God surely would, too? If this was the case, what shape did you—do you—think God's abandonment of you would take? Would you expect to be left unable to take care of yourself financially or emotionally? Did you—do you—feel that doom is hanging over your head ready to drop if you don't watch out? Do you simply feel cosmically unlovable? What laws did you work out about the universe that you decided you must live by if you were not to be abandoned in it?

Now ask yourself how what you worked out as a child fit with and reinforced what you learned about God at church, at home, from Bible stories, or from the other children. For myself, I remember very well the moment when I discovered in my prayer that as a child

I had more or less permanently joined into one piece my need to be loyal to my mother in her suffering after my parents' divorce, my cultural expectations about women and suffering, and everything I had heard about how good Jesus was for suffering in our place. Having made the connection, without even being aware of it, I had accepted for myself that happiness was not something available to me. What God demanded of me, if I were to be accepted by God, was lifelong suffering and, in short, depression. How about yourself? If you can put your finger on a particular Christian teaching, or Bible stories or Bible verses that intersected and gave you an explanation for the rest of your life in this way, you are already a long way to healing.

Blessedly, I have found that sometimes, just sometimes, such a discovery as this and healing come simultaneously. Usually there is nothing terribly dramatic about such healing; it simply happens that, in the moment when I am able to see what I've actually been believing in my heart, I am also able to say, "In my head, I really do know better than this already. Now my heart can hear it, too."

Occasionally, particularly when I have been pushed to utter despair about ever coming through on the other side of whatever it is that I am wrestling with, healing insight comes much more dramatically, as a kind of blinding revelation of God. Certainly this was true for me in the case I just told you about. At the very same moment when I saw how I had connected my experience and my theology around the question of women and suffering I was able to know that what I had believed was false. So, a new-old truth was put in place of what I had believed from childhood. As the words of the Easter liturgy, "the joy of the resurrection fills the whole world," rang in my head, the grace of God flooded me. It was as though my brain were suddenly rewired. As my lifelong depression came to its end, I could really understand that the whole point of the work of Jesus is not crucifixion and suffering but resurrection and joy.[3]

The sudden way my lifelong depression came to an end after all the years of work I had done on it strikes me with wonder and gratitude to this day. Still, I don't want to mislead you. This is not the way it usually happens for me. Rather, the whole process of discovery, of finding the exact point of intersection between my theology and my experience, and most especially being able to substitute a new, true theology for the old, false one, takes a long time.

In fact, here, in seeking a way for the heart to hear and assimilate a new theology in the place of the old, we get to some of the hardest work of prayer yet and the most need for patience and stubbornness. Where do we look for help? How should you, my friend, go about

---

3. See chapter 5 of *Memories of God* for a more complete account of what happened in this long process.

actively looking? The most obvious place is in scripture; in fact, this is one of the strongest arguments for reading the Bible for a bit every day. If you already have a practice of praying the psalms or reading a little from one of the Gospels as part of your everyday prayer, sooner or later, if you are seeking a solution to a specific problem of the sort we have been talking about, the chances are you will hear the healing words you need through scripture itself. Then, you can get to work and follow up on them.

I remember once, at a time when I was really wrestling with feeling excluded by the official maleness of the Christian tradition, being so goaded by the oppressive male language of the psalms that I finally got really angry at God. After a few weeks of suffering through this, it came to me that what I needed was to direct my attention to all the places where the psalms stated quite clearly that, wherever the historical church had stood and still stands on this matter, God's own preference was not for the status quo and those in power but for those who, as I perceived myself to be, were excluded from it. My spirits lifted almost immediately, but my work with scripture wasn't over. From here my job—as it will be yours when you get to this point—was first to try to identify what I had been thinking Jesus had taught about this, and then, second, to look at the gospels to see what Jesus really did have to say. Believe me, when I looked at what Jesus said about the status quo, there was a lot there, and it was just about all negative.

Sometimes, however, scripture either is not helpful to me or it does not supply me with everything I need. Then I turn for conversation to some of the texts and teachers that have been the most illuminating or freeing for me in the past. For myself, this generally means *The Sayings of the Fathers* of early monasticism and the writings of Dorotheos of Gaza. As for you, you have told me repeatedly over the years how Julian of Norwich has spoken words of grace to you. When you find yourself in this position, it is time to go back and re-read her with your questions.

And speaking of conversation, never forget that the tradition you are drawing on does not lie only in the past in some dead and fixed form. Be sure to talk with friends or spouse or colleagues or former teachers or a therapist you trust about what it is with which you are wrestling. Surely, they will often be faithful transmitters of the gospel for you. If they know you well, they will tell you what they think they've observed about you that will expand your knowledge of yourself, both how you have been and how you want to be. Still, don't expect that, in order to be helpful to you, these people ought to have the answers, or necessarily even understand you. Perhaps by their saying the very opposite of what you need, you will hit on the solution. There is no telling from whom God's word of grace will come in a form you can actually hear it. There is just something about what the ancient teachers called "consultation" with the sisters or brothers that can open the eyes and the heart.

All of this so far falls in the category of active, intelligent seeking. In addition there is another necessary and simultaneous kind of seeking that is not so directly active. I could describe it as passive, but it isn't really. More than anything else, this second kind of seeking consists in a commitment to paying attention to whatever comes to us and before us in the expectation that everything belonging to God and being full of the glory of God—the familiar prayers of the liturgy, a dream, the neighbor's dog, an article in a newspaper, an exchange in the grocery store with a stranger—can reveal to us what we need to know. I have found over the years, for example, that in certain circumstances, just praying the Lord's Prayer regularly without really concentrating on it has allowed the words to become alive for me in a special way so that it speaks just what I need. This has been true repeatedly for me with particular sayings from *The Sayings of the Fathers*.

Now, let's assume that you are finally coming to see things differently. You are close to the end of the work of your prayer, but you are not quite finished. The last thing you will want to do is to go back over what you have discovered and try to construct what you have learned into the story of your life. To give you the focus you need, make use of the particular lens of loss or resurrection or trust, or whatever it is you have been working on. If possible, find someone else to whom to tell your story. Perhaps write it down to keep for your-self and go back to later.

Notice that I am not really making a distinction be-tween using a personal issue, like your difficulty with loss, as a lens for telling your story, and using a theological issue like crucifixion and resurrection. If you have gone through this whole process we've been talking about in your prayer, the theological and the experiential will come together. Also notice that I am not suggesting that you try to tell the whole story of your life. There will be plenty of details that will not fit into what you are looking at here, and it will only distract from the task. Rather, you are telling it only from the single perspective you've been considering. Believe me, by the time you draw into your story the other relevant events and ideas and patterns and theological convictions in your life, you will have just about as much material as you can handle at once.

Here is a gentle warning. Constructing this kind of narrative is as hard as any of the other work you will have been doing in your prayer, and I know that, having gotten so far already, you may be tempted to skip doing this last "storytelling" part. I promise you, my friend, if you persist, you will be glad you did. In doing this for myself, I have never failed to learn much more than I already knew about how the themes I had been working with really had shaped and been extended into all sorts of areas of my life I hadn't recognized. Even more important, however, I have also never failed to discover in the past and present pain the ways and places "grace has brought me safe thus far," and I have been filled over and over again with a sense of wonder at and gratitude for the gift of my own life.

Let me say one more thing before I close, and that is that I know that you worry about prayer being "too subjective," too much the result of our own mental processes that we then ascribe to God. You know, my friend, that there is no form of prayer where this isn't going to be something to worry about. You will simply have to judge the truthfulness of your experience of it on the basis of the promise of the gospel. If you are able to live in a wider world of trust, if you have come closer to learning that God will not abandon you, if you are braver, if it fits with what you know of scripture, if you are more willing to take risks to love and be loved, if you are less afraid of life, if you experience yourself as more real and less living in fantasy or in principle, if you are eager to continue the work of prayer, and if you long for God in new ways, this is the only proof of its truthfulness you are likely to have.

My good friend, this is as much as I can tell you right now about how to do the healing work of prayer. I hope that you'll find what you are looking for in it. I'm sure you'll ask me whatever you need to. Know that, as always, you are in my heart.

*Roberta*

# A Silver Flute,
# a Blue Steel Sorrow

*My dear friend,*

I was so glad to get your letter last week. I'm sorry you are having so much trouble wrestling with those old intractable things of your childhood. I know that it doesn't help much to realize that almost all of us have things from our childhoods that bind us and continue to give us pain in our adult lives.

In an earlier letter I noted that we so often hear people say that if we only turn our pain over to God, we will be at peace. I'm sure there may be some for whom it could work like this, but for most of us I don't think it is so simple or so easy as that. For myself, I've learned the hard way that "turning over" childhood stuff to God might in theory be wonderfully helpful if I could actually do it, but I can't imagine, practically speaking, how I would do it. My own experience, coupled with my early monastic teachers, tells me that the work of healing is generally a pretty slow and painful business. It's not nearly so passive a process as that "turning over" language seems to suggest, either.

At any rate, you said in your letter that what you hoped for in my next letter was an actual description of what I had been working on in my own prayer. You wanted to know what exactly I had been doing, and what I had learned while I was doing it that might be helpful to you. I am glad to do what you ask. Though I know that we are very different in our ways of prayer— we are unalike in so many other ways, how could it be otherwise?—I hope with my whole heart that you will find something of God here in my account to help you, too. I quoted the wonderful desert father Poemen in my last letter as he used to say that "not understanding what has happened prevents us from going forward."[1] Because I have found him to be right more often than not, I will ask you to be patient with me when I start my account back as far as four years ago.

✻ ✻ ✻ ✻ ✻ ✻ ✻ ✻ ✻ ✻ ✻ ✻ ✻ ✻ ✻ ✻ ✻ ✻ ✻ ✻ ✻ ✻ ✻ ✻ ✻ ✻ ✻ ✻ ✻ ✻ ✻ ✻ ✻ ✻ ✻ ✻ ✻

It was a hard year the year I got my second flute. It was on Holy Thursday of that same spring that my father died, and in September my mother very nearly

---

1. Poemen 200, *Sayings of the Desert Fathers,* trans. Ward, p. 194.

died, too, of emergency heart bypass surgery. I suppose I'm not likely ever to know the exact cause of my decision to go out and buy myself an instrument when I did. I know it had something to do with turning fifty that November, but that wasn't all there was to it.

I had gotten my first flute, the flute I had before the new one, immediately after my parents were divorced and my mother, two little brothers, and I moved to my grandparents' farm in Kentucky. I was almost twelve. I had longed for an instrument to play, a way to make music, for a long time before that, but my father had forbidden it. He had made it plain that I was not the sort of child it was worth spending family money on. I was too lazy, too stubbornly unwilling to do anything I did the right way, too unlikely to finish anything I started to be trusted to practice. His explicit, articulated judgment had shamed me utterly, and I had grieved.

I had grieved, and because I grieved my mother had grieved with me. This is why, even in her disastrous financial condition, one of the first things she did after her divorce was to buy a flute and to arrange for music lessons. I remember still the joy with which the very sight of that flute filled me then, the gleam of its silver in the case and the weight of its long body balanced in my hands. I also remember the longing I had that went with it that I, somehow, would not turn out to be with my flute the person my father had judged me to be.

Of course I did turn out that way. Part of it was that I had terrible trouble with depression as a child (this was not something that people acknowledged to be possible in those days), and so I really was undisciplined and too tired to do much of anything most of the time. Another part was the utter panic that would hit me every time I came to something I couldn't understand, or even that I couldn't play right the first time I tried it. The origin of that panic was my conviction that my father had passed judgment once and for all on who I was. Now, I could never escape that judgment. I was a person who should not and did not deserve to play the flute. I was a girl who couldn't and wouldn't learn.

Still, I persisted in my undisciplined playing right through high school, and I loved it guiltily. The sounds that I made filled me with something that was more than pleasure. Certainly what I felt was a kind of happiness, even joy, that I experienced nowhere else. Though I didn't practice, and I wasn't skilled, I played a lot. I loved playing duets with my friend Mary Ann, who played viola; I loved marching band; I loved being in the Louisville Youth Orchestra.

What I couldn't do, however, was to shake either my shame at who I seemed to myself to be or my grief over the loss of my father, who had left us. At eighteen, convinced that somehow marriage would allow me to escape everything about myself I hated, I married. My failure to play well had proved my father right. In spite of my love of it, or perhaps especially because of my love of it, it was time to give up to my father's judgment. I sold my flute.

So much happened in my life in the years that followed; college, seminary, graduate school, children, teaching, divorce, and remarriage, and all of it without music that I made myself, or even music that I much listened to, since listening would fill me with a sadness that was inexplicable to me at the time. What could have happened, then, thirty-two years later, that made me decide to buy another flute?

Again, it had a lot to do with my father. Not surprisingly, most of my adult life we had had a painful relationship. Though I had loved him very much, we had not seen each other often, and when we had, I had always felt self-conscious and stupid in his presence. Then, around the time I turned forty I was given some work to do that took me three or four times a year to New York City, where he lived. At the urging of my dear aunt, his sister, and the desert fathers and mothers who had long been my teachers in prayer, I decided to visit him.

The first visit was painful, but it was surprising and wonderful, too. He had emphysema now, and I was astounded to see that he had learned a kind of gentleness and humility that I had never known him to have before. He was glad to see me; it was clear to me at once that, as I had missed him and longed for him over the years, he had also missed me. In the years that followed, I stayed with him whenever I came to New York, and in that time we came to know, appreciate, and love each other very much.

About a year before he died, as we were talking in his little den, he asked me whether I ever played my flute anymore.

"Oh no," I answered him. "I sold it when I was eighteen."

"I'm so sorry to hear that," he replied. "Do you think you could still play? I remember the way the sound of your playing would go right through me and make me shiver. It was so beautiful."

"Beautiful!" I was too astounded even to answer him. My only memory connecting my father with my flute was the shaming conversation that had governed so much of my life since then. I didn't even have the flute till after my parents were divorced. How could he possibly have heard me play? But in spite of my memories, he must have heard me, and he didn't remember judging me in the way I would have expected him to. All that he could recall was that it had been beautiful to him.

My grief when he died the next year was awful, yet it seemed to me at the time that my gratitude for the mysterious healing that had come to our relationship in the short years preceding his death was even stronger than my grief. It was in that state of grief, gratitude, and what felt like a new kind of experience of adulthood that I decided several months later on my fiftieth birthday, without really giving myself a reason, to buy the flute.

What an amazing thing getting that flute was! If playing my original flute had filled me with happiness so long ago, it was nothing to what I experienced now. From the first night, I found that though my flute-playing muscles and my physical skills were long gone, I could remember the notes, the fingerings, and enough of the way I needed to hold my mouth to play real music.

For the first month I hardly let that flute out of my sight. I heard the sounds of it every night in my sleep, and when it wasn't at my mouth, I thought about it. During much of the whole first two years I had it, it seemed to me that every time I played the Holy Spirit sang and soared in me in great swoops of joy and delight. It was like being crazy in love, drunk with love.

But I did say it was for "much of the whole first two years," because there was something else, besides my joy, that was going on with my flute playing that was very frightening. A month after my birthday I had begun to take lessons. Now, as I once again found myself sometimes unable to understand what I was asked to do, and sometimes was still unable to do what I was asked even after I had tried to practice it, I became again the child I had once been. My new joy began to alternate with my old panic and shame that had come back with a vengeance to torture me, as though those thirty-two years separating my childhood from my adulthood had never intervened.

I fought for myself in every way I knew. I considered that I was no longer the child I had been, that I had a good and new adult life in which I experienced myself as competent personally and professionally. I reminded myself of what my father had said about my playing before he died. I paid very close attention to the desert fathers and mothers who in my mind were telling me daily on the one hand that I was passing judgment on myself that I had no business to pass, and on the other, that what I was fighting against were unrealistic expectations of myself that were completely at odds with the goals that I wanted to accomplish. "Think small," they kept repeating to me. "Learning to play again is like the successful practice of any other virtue. It depends upon the expectation that you will encounter serious trouble along the way, that you will only make progress slowly. How can you possibly think otherwise?"

Of course, I believed them in my head. My heart, however, was another matter. "What if I can't learn?" I would whisper fearfully to them in return. "What if my father was right? What if I love my flute this much and I really can't learn?"

"You can learn," they would answer me patiently in my imagination, "but you are fifty years old. You cannot learn in the same way you could when you were fifteen. Accept what you have now as the good gift of God. Haven't you learned anything from us over the years about what humility really means? You have this trouble most when you won't accept your limits, but everybody has limits. You must not give in to your demoralization; you must discipline yourself to keep on going in the face of your shame and your panic."

I took what they recommended as my spiritual discipline directed against my own perfectionism and despair, and I followed their advice daily for two years. At the end of the two years, after practicing about an hour a day, demoralized or not, I found that I really had made progress. My conviction that I *could* actually learn by practicing, if I worked hard at it, had grown greatly. My periods of despair, though I still had them, had grown shorter and a bit less debilitating. At the same time, I became prepared to accept that they would never entirely go away, and that I would simply have to live with what remained of them.

Then, just as I began to believe that, just by gritting my teeth, I had gotten over the biggest part of the hump of all of this, I learned otherwise. Though I hadn't realized it before, in the same way my grief over the death of my father had been made easier by the extravagance of my gratitude for receiving him back in my middle age, now I discovered the way in which my grief over the loss of my flute had been eased by my gratitude at its return.

One morning, for no particular reason I can name, I woke up to discover that in the night my gratitude for the return of my flute had been stripped away and all that was left behind was grief. Now, before I emptied my first cup of coffee I found myself overwhelmed with a vivid knowledge of the cost that I had paid all those entire thirty-two years of my adult life, the years of my twenties, my thirties, and my forties, by living without music. At the same time I was consumed with what the great monastic teacher Evagrius Ponticus describes as the passion of regret—bitter, corrosive longing for what might have been[2]—I was also consumed with scorn and anger at the self that had made this choice.

Those first moments of realization that day were not pleasant, nor were they quickly over. Though the intensity of my feelings came and went like bouts of malaria, over the next two years my anger, grief, and regret did not go away. During this time I struggled with them in my prayer and outside of it as best I could, but even with the good help of my old teachers, the Ammas and Abbas of the desert, my regret and anger remained as intractable as winter in the Arctic, as indigestible as steel. I could

---

2. Evagrius also calls this passion "sadness." See the Praktikos, 10 in *The Praktikos,* Chapters on Prayer, trans. John E. Bamberger, O.C.S.O., Cistercian Studies, 1970, p. 17.

find no real way to figure what I needed to do in order to make progress.

Then, this past Easter week, something of all this began to break open in my prayer. It began on Holy Thursday, the day four years earlier on which my father had died. During my prayer that morning I had unexpectedly been seized by a strong visual image: I found myself standing in the middle of a clearing in a winter woods looking at a long, low, flat-roofed building made entirely of the dull blue steel of knives. Somehow, in the way of dreams or prayer I knew that my father was in the building. I was desperate to reach him, but there was no way I could get inside because in the whole of the building there was neither a door nor a window. On every side its walls and roof were as smooth as glass.

Then, as I stood there pondering what I was seeing, the image faded and I was returned to the familiar space of my prayer, only to find that something had happened to me. I no longer felt the same way about my father as I had felt a few minutes earlier. As the comfort of my gratitude for the return of my flute had gone, my gratitude for those last years of happiness with my father was gone as well. Now without the benefit of its soothing presence, I found myself knocked down by a fresh, raw grief for the loss of my father the likes of which I had never known before.

Somehow, in impenetrable pain that was physical as much as it was mental, I got through the work and the conversations of that day. It was a relief that my prayer the next morning, which was Good Friday, contained no images. Then, on Holy Saturday, the day four years earlier on which my father had joined Jesus in the tomb, almost as soon as I sat down in my red chair for my prayers I found myself back at the building of steel. This time, however, I was inside the building; it was very damp and cold and strongly smelled of decaying oak leaves. Though I couldn't see the walls for the impenetrable darkness, I knew I was standing in the center of the room, and I was looking down at the body of my father, who was stretched out on a kind of platform resting on two sawhorses. A pair of thick red candles in tall stands flickered at his head and feet.

I stood there a few moments looking at him without touching him. Then, once again the image faded and I was returned to myself in even more grief and pain than I had known the two days before. This time, however, rather than the generalized grief of loss I had felt on the previous days, what I was experiencing now was very specific: it was grief for myself over what it had meant to be my father's daughter in the time of my childhood, grief for the ways he had hurt me by the things he had done and said, for the ways he had left me, for the long years in which he had seemed to me to be indifferent to my existence.

The pain of this new grief persisted through the rest of that day; and the next, which was Easter, was just the same. That year, it seemed, Easter had passed me by. I arose on Monday to find that my grief was as fresh as it had been the day before.

That morning, I sat down drearily for my prayer, full of self-pity and expecting nothing. Then, a third time, all at once I found myself back with the building in the woods. Now, however, several things had changed. For one thing, the season was different; where on the two previous days it had been winter, it had become early spring. For another, I was standing in a different place; I was in a dirt road which ran up to the building, rather than in a clearing in the woods. But most important, I could see that where only four days ago the surface of the metal structure had had the appearance of oiled blue steel, it was now covered with dull red rust. Its flat steel roof was collapsing inward, and there were gaps at the corners wide enough for a person to fit through.

Confused, I walked up the road and squeezed through a corner of the building. By the thin spring sunlight coming through the cracks in the ceiling I looked cautiously for my father. My father, the bier, and the candles all were gone. Empty of anything but drifts of leathery brown leaves, the building gave every appearance of having been deserted long ago. Puzzled and a little afraid, I turned to go, wondering if I had made up everything that I had originally thought I had seen.

Then, it occurred to me to brush aside the leaves in the middle of the floor. Sure enough, there, just where it should have been, were the hardened pools of candle wax, fresh and red like blood.

Inexplicably, that Monday, when this last image faded and my attention returned to the red chair in my study in which I sat, the sharpness of my grief for my father seemed to have faded with it. In the next few days I wondered what it was that had really occurred within me. Was my old grief really gone, or, as sometimes happens, were the images in my prayer a kind of promise of God of what would come to me if I did the work that was about to come before me?

I did not begin to find out the answer to this question until several months later in the middle of the summer when a series of events in my family intensely stirred up again the old anxieties and fears that sieze me when I feel myself to be threatened with the loss of anyone I love. Surprisingly to me, along with those familiar fears came, not the old expected grief for my father, but rather the magnified and equally familiar panic and shame with which I had wrestled so ineffectively, relatively speaking, so hard and so recently with respect to my flute.

Why was I experiencing these feelings of panic and shame in what felt like such an unrelated place? I couldn't understand it, and I knew I could no longer live with all these wounds that had hurt me for so long in the form I was experiencing them. Though the time was wrong for me in terms of the other work of my life, this was work for my prayer I could not choose to set aside until later.

For myself, I only know one way to do this work. I began by trying to figure out exactly what it was that was hurting me so that, in the safe space of God's presence, I could dredge up the relevant childhood memories connected with its origins and seek healing. Fighting against my own panic even to identify the area in which I needed to work took several days.

Then one morning I woke up able to see where my work lay: it had come to me in the night that in all the years I had never even talked to my husband about the things connected with the events surrounding my parents' divorce, or my feelings around that time. Now, it seemed to me that, though I did not remember making such a decision, at some level I must have decided long ago that facing the pain of that time directly would simply hurt too much. If I were ever to get past the place where I was, however, I knew I needed now to go ahead and face the whole of it.

Still, to face it and to find what else was back there in that time that was governing me now, I needed a way back into it. I needed a memory that could be a door for me. Once having acknowledged this need to myself,

I asked God for a memory connected with that time. The memory came quickly.

The next morning at the end of my prayer, I suddenly found myself in my mind standing in my parents' silent living room a week or so before we children and my mother abandoned the house in Delaware where we had lived for a year to move to Kentucky. The house was unnaturally silent; I was by myself, and I was desolate. The closed gray drapes muffled the drab afternoon sunlight, but not enough to prevent me from seeing the taped-up moving boxes piled in the center of the room. I was not, however, attending to the boxes; they were nothing more than background to the central image that was gripping me that morning in my prayer.

What I was looking at in that dim room was a plant of my mother's sitting to the left in a long plant stand on the floor under the window. It was a large crown of thorns that she had moved with us from New York City the year before. Its single bony-looking sharp-thorned gray-green stem was covered with little round leaves; sinister tiny red-centered white flowers grew directly out of the trunk. As if this were not enough, the topmost tip of the plant had been tied to the bottom of the stem with a frayed white rag to hold it in place. During the course of that long year in Delaware the whole plant had been trained by my mother into the shape of Jesus' crown. I had always thought it ugly; now it was the ugliest thing

I had ever seen. The very sight of it filled me with loathing and a sick feeling in the pit of my stomach.

Whether I really had once stood there looking at that crown of thorns in just this way at that time, I have no way to tell. I know my mother did indeed have such a plant and that I truly hated it. I also know that there was something in my memory of that crown of thorns that brought with it a whole complexity of other memories, not only of what I had felt on that long-ago day preceding our move to Kentucky, but also what I had experienced in the months, and even years, that came later.

Most of what came back to me in my prayer that day seemed hardly bearable. I again experienced as an almost-twelve-year-old my confusion and sharp grief over the loss of my father. I felt again in a way I never before had acknowledged to myself the vibrating intensity of my love for my father. I felt my crushing shame that my father, who had already found me unworthy in so many other ways, was now leaving me definitively because of my unworthiness. Then, below everything else, I found and recognized the same fierce guilty anger, scorn, and hatred I had recently been feeling toward the self who had sold my first flute and abandoned music.

Now, I thought at the end of my prayer that day, on the basis of past experience, I should start to feel better. For the first time, it seemed to me, I had all the pieces I needed to understand and address these devastating memories directly in my prayer. I could see now, rationally, that I had interpreted my father's leaving as a deliberate rejection of my love and myself as unworthy. I could actually recall deciding as a twelve-year-old that, if my father did not want the child I was, then I did not want her, either. Even more terrible, I had discovered in myself, and I wept when I discovered it, that even as an adult I had continued to accept both that twelve-year-old's interpretation of what had happened with my parents' divorce and the twelve-year-old's scorn and hatred of that child she was as well. I knew now that it was this—the sentence of scorn and hatred that child once and for all had passed on me—it was this that was at the root of my recurring panic and despair over my ability to play my flute, and was also at the root of my fears that by my unworthiness I would finally force all those I loved to leave me.

The fact was, however, that past experience or not, the discovery of where all this had come from brought with it a certain relief, but it did not make it go away. Indeed, I was still left with the problem of what I was to do with these awful feelings and judgments that had periodically risen up from the groundwater of my life for so long.

I started to take on the problem by using the brain that God had given me. Not as the child I had been but as an intelligent and informed adult, I began to sort out the difference between what the child had thought had happened with my parents' divorce and what actually must have happened. I was able to remember how, after many months, my mother had told me that, though my father really had left me, in his own mind it was not I he had left but rather, my mother. My being left was only a kind of by-product of that other leaving. Now, for the first time I could actually believe it.

At the same time, I was also able to acknowledge that there was a real layer of truth in my childhood perception of my relationship with my father and the way that he had scorned my adoration of him as worth nothing to him. The truth was this: Though he actually had loved me, what I most experienced as a child was the fact that I had continually irritated him. Now I could admit to myself that he really had not been able to cope with any of his children while they were growing up. His irritation had surely not been directed at me personally any more than it would have been at any child who had been in my place.

Still, even after I had had time to mull over these new insights, I found that all was not much better than it had been before. Indeed, in spite of everything, it was yet the case that the bulk of my pain, my confusion of the shame my younger self had long ago experienced with my present self's shame had not left me, nor had my virulent adult rejection of the child I had been. Rather, my very consciousness of all this now rose up in me as increased panic and anger toward that twelve-year-old child. The outward, visible sign of my panic and anger was this: I absolutely did not even want to pick up the flute which had by now been my daily companion for four whole years.

Fortunately for me, or rather, I should say blessedly, in whatever we are doing or wherever we may think we are in our prayer, God never ceases to work in us. One day after I first remembered my mother's crown of thorns I was truly given a great gift in my prayer. It had not been a good morning. I had wrestled with all this throughout the time I had spent in my prayer, and had gotten no help.

Then, all of a sudden, with no warning, I heard myself praying the familiar words of the Lord's Prayer, and in a way entirely new to me. I was not praying out of what I knew that Jesus must have meant by it in first-century Palestine. Instead, I was repeating each phrase of the prayer out of these modern experiences of my own life, and I was praying as though my life depended on it, which of course, it did. After each phrase I was articulating both exactly what it meant to me in that moment, and on the basis of that, exactly what I understood I needed to ask God for. It was wonderful; it was like sitting down to food and drink when you are starving.

*"Our father,"* I began, and as I said *"our"* my soul came entirely to attention. I had long studied the com-

mentary on the Lord's Prayer of Cyprian, the great third-century teacher of the North African Church, and he was there with me that day to offer me saving help. Remember when we pray this prayer, he was reminding me now, we do not pray "my father," by ourselves, but rather, we pray it together with all our brothers and sisters in Christ.

"All our sisters in Christ!" What I had never let myself acknowledge before was that, however my adult self felt about it, that child I'd been actually was my sister in Christ, and that, moreover, to God, that child was and still is as much God's beloved child as I, the adult Roberta, am. Now, for the first time, I knew without any doubt that this was so, and that moreover, God was relieving me of the burden of accepting that child as my sister simply by putting the words "our Father" into my mouth to pray for both her and me at the same time.

So, I prayed that day, "Our father—my father and the father of that child I cannot either escape or forgive—I accept that you, at any rate, love us both equally as your children."

"*Who art in heaven,*" I heard myself say after that; then, "I know that it is a very strange idea in the everyday world I live in, but I have learned both from my teachers of the early church and from my own experience that the Communion of the Saints is very real. In you the past is never really past. Rather, in you and in your eternity all time is simultaneous. But this means that in you the child I was not only is still as alive as she ever was, but also, that in you I can talk to her and care for her, confront her directly with my questions and my anger. Even more, I know that if I am willing to try, I can seek healing for both of us, and moreover, expect to receive it. On the other hand, this being willing business is not such an easy thing for me.

*"Hallowed be your name,"* I said next, and as I said it I recalled again my teacher Cyprian, who had reminded his third-century congregation in Carthage that because God's name is already holy, what Jesus must have intended us to ask for here was that God's name be made holy *in us.*

Holy in us! I groaned. I had long ago been convinced that, through the very fact of the persistence of the image of God in all human beings, God is already made holy in every person. My prayer had suddenly become too hard for me as I realized that next, I had to ask to see the presence of God's holiness and goodness in that child I had been. I knew very well that I didn't want to see it now or at any time, or to know it, either. If I did see it, how could I continue to hate that child and maintain my safe distance from her?

God, whose ways of grace are too wonderful for me, had caught me in a snare I could not escape. I groaned again. "Hallowed be your name," I prayed. "I am willing for you to show me your holy presence in that child I was."

"*Your kingdom come,*" I prayed after that. "According to Jesus' own teaching, not to mention the psalms that I have been praying for such a long time, the world is not the way you intend it to be, but clearly your intention and your promise is that you will set all things right. This is good news I need to hear. It is really different from what my father taught me as a child and what I am fighting against so hard in myself—that I am unable to do anything right, and that, furthermore, unless I do everything just the way it ought to be done, then there is no point in doing it at all."

"*Your* kingdom come," I prayed, "so that I can live in it and no longer live in the kingdom my father as a young man never meant to establish in me, the kingdom that, at the end of his life, was no longer even familiar to him."

"*Your will be done*" were the next words of my prayer. "My God," I prayed, "I know that when I am demoralized and full of panic and grief, I am tempted to believe that my pain is somehow your will, your desired punishment for my failures. I really do know how gently you regard all our wounds, all the things that hurt us. Certainly, you never desire our deaths, but how hard I find it to make myself remember this when

I feel bad! It puts what I learned so well as a childhood survival skill in terrible tension with what you desire for me, and that tension makes me feel unsafe and sometimes even crazy.

"Our God, because I can't seem to retain it for myself, I need you to remind me constantly that what you desire for all people, including for me and for little Roberta, is our well-being and our health.

"*Give us this day our daily bread,*" next was my prayer. "My God," I went on, "I know my needs and the needs of the child I was are great. It is so hard for me even now to see them as real and valid because I inadvertently learned as a child that they were not. Now I fill up with panic whenever I believe that I will not have what I need in the way of abilities, skills, or emotional resources to do what I must do. I am trying to hear you reassure me that, in spite of my experiences as a child, I already have a good deal of what I need, and what I don't have, you will faithfully and reliably supply if I only ask for it.

"Therefore, I am asking you with my whole heart to give us, little Roberta and grown Roberta, not forever but for today, between now and bedtime, the things we need to live and thrive.

"*Forgive us our sins, as we forgive those who sin against us,*" I began to pray after that before I realized that I had once again fallen into God's trap of grace. I hated to pray these next words so much that it made my heart race and sweat stand out on my forehead. Because I hurt, I prayed them anyway.

"I know that your *actual forgiveness* of the injuries I've done myself and the child I was do not depend upon the forgiving that I do, but I do know that my ability to *experience* your forgiveness does. A desire for this experience of forgiveness is not a noble reason for my attempt to forgive that child, but it is the best I can do right now.

"I am asking you to help me to forgive the child I was for whatever part she had in driving away my father. At the same time, help me understand that, even if our father in his youth really didn't have much use for her, she wasn't lazy, careless, or unable to do anything right. Against terrible odds, she was doing the best she could.

"And, our loving God, I am also asking you to help me in your eternal present to repent and confess to the living child I was how badly I have treated her. I have hated her and blamed her for nearly everything that has gone on in my adult life as though she had somehow deliberately made choices for me that, in fact, she never meant to make. Please, God of both of us, enable her to forgive me, so that all, my childhood self and my adult self, may be one in you.

"*Lead us not into temptation and deliver us from evil*" came after that, and these words I could pray fervently. "When I am in one of those familiar situations of panic and shame, I am so tempted just to give myself up to the feelings and not fight for myself. Then I want to punish the child I was and the adult I am, too. This really is evil, and I need you to rescue me from it."

At last, I had said everything I had to say, and so I concluded, "My God, it seems to me that I am asking you for a lot, but I ask it all confidently. I am able to ask it, partly because it was Jesus who taught me to pray this prayer, but also because I know that you really can give me what I ask, that *'yours is the kingdom'*—that all these things are in your kind and generous hands, that *'yours is the power'*—that you want to and have the power to give to me the things I pray for, and that finally, *'yours is the glory,'* and I have seen it myself lying over all things you have created like a shining veil of light, *'forever and ever.'* I ask all these things in the name of your love."

Then, with my whole heart, I said *"Amen."*

＊ ＊ ＊ ＊ ＊ ＊ ＊ ＊ ＊ ＊ ＊ ＊ ＊ ＊ ＊ ＊ ＊ ＊ ＊ ＊ ＊ ＊ ＊ ＊ ＊ ＊ ＊ ＊ ＊ ＊ ＊ ＊ ＊ ＊ ＊ ＊ ＊ ＊ ＊ ＊ ＊ ＊

My friend, it would be so satisfying to tell you that when I got up from my prayer that morning, the process of healing I had been undergoing for so long was complete, but of course, it wasn't. What I can say with confidence, however, is this: When my prayers were over that day I felt myself to have been deeply satisfied by the God who had taught me how to pray. At the same time,

I had become confident that if I were only faithful in my prayer and if I were to persist in doing the long-term work of it, the new way to pray that I had been given really would continue to bring slow and steady healing.

So far, after praying in this way now for a number of months, I seem to have been proven right, and here for me is a single proof. Yesterday I attended the flute recital of the fourteen-year-old daughter of a friend of mine. When, after hearing her play, I realized that she had made more progress in half a year than I had made in the whole of my previous four years, I did not fall into despair and decide, as I had so often before, that I had no business playing the flute. Instead, I felt melancholy for a while. Then, I reminded myself that, though it is true that I will never play half so well as I would have if I hadn't given it up in the first place, still when I do play, I play in the very kingdom I pray for daily. Here, the pleasure my flute gives me is the pleasure of God.

Blessings, my friend, on your own work. I will wait eagerly to hear from you. With love,

*Roberta*

# Dancing Babycakes

*My dear friend,*

In your last letter you observe that, whatever else I say in my letters about prayer, an awful lot of my own issues over the years seem to you to have been resolved by what I call my prayer images. You ask me, therefore, to tell me more about them. In reply, I must say that I haven't talked explicitly about prayer images much because they are neither necessary to prayer, nor does everybody have them.

More specifically, however, I have not wanted to make you anxious if you don't happen to be one of those people who do have them. Now I see that I have been right to be concerned because you tell me in your letter that you are afraid that you won't be able to find healing in your prayer without them. Oh, my friend, if only it weren't so hard to believe that the prayer of each of us is merely different, not better or worse, than the prayer of anybody else! But you know, it really is true. You don't need prayer images to do this work. As my early church teachers insist, God comes to each of us and brings saving help in the way best suited to the very individual people we are.

Still, since the idea of these images is making you anxious, I will do as you ask and say a little more about what prayer images are like for me and how I think about them. After that, however, I intend to give you an example of something important I've been working on in my prayer over the last year that hasn't involved prayer images at all. Then you will be able to see for yourself that I mean it when I say that the healing work of prayer doesn't depend for me on these experiences.

Now, I will try to answer some of your questions about prayer images. To begin, you ask in your letter if they are something like dreams. I can only answer that in some ways they are, and in other ways they are not. Do you remember the image of the field and the apple tree I wrote you about a while ago? Both in terms of the visual content of that image and in terms of my experience of all the physical sensations of standing in a cold rainy field, it was very much like a kind of intense dream that is so vivid that the light, color, textures, and sensations of the waking world seem drab and washed out in comparison.

This isn't always the case with prayer images, however. Sometimes the visual element in these images has actually been pretty faint or indistinct—almost the idea of an image rather than a true visual image. Occasionally, a prayer image will contain no actual visual element at all. Certainly it happened like this when my depression was brought to an end by hearing the words "the joy of the resurrection renews the whole world" resounding in my head.[1]

One way prayer images and dreams differ is that while the prayer images are occurring I am never asleep; rather, I am nearly always in a special state of alertness that continues right through the experience into the time that follows it. The image of the field came to me, for example, immediately before I had to lecture to a hundred and fifty people. It did not in any way interfere with what I did. In fact, feeling present in my own skin to an unusual degree, and being full of the energy of what I had just learned, I imagine I gave a bit better lecture than usual.

Another significant thing about these prayer images that you have noted yourself is this: Though they often come at the beginning of some significant work that lies before me in my prayer (as was the case with the image

---

1. *Memories of God,* chapter 4.

of the field) they more commonly occur at the end of the work at the point when I have just about despaired that I can ever conclude it.

Oddly, when the prayer images do come under these circumstances, they bring with them a paradox. On the one hand, the sudden freeing insights that accompany them always seem to me to be at the same time entirely new and entirely familiar. What they tell me is something I have never been able to work out for myself; at the same time, I am sure that there is nothing new in the image that I haven't known in my head all along.

The way the words "the joy of the resurrection renews the whole world" brought an end to my lifelong depression is a good example of this paradox. I had wrestled with that depression for so long! Without such a clear prayer image, I don't think I could ever have figured out that what was holding me in my depression was my unrecognized conviction that, if I were really to love other people, I must live in a continuous state of crucifixion. Yet, at the same time, I am sure that there must never really have been a time when I did not know in my head that the end and point of the Christian life is not crucifixion but resurrection.

But, I can hear you asking, couldn't everything you've said so far apply to dreams, too? Yes, I suppose so, insofar as dreams often untie knots we couldn't seem to untie without them. This is precisely why I think we have to learn to pay more attention to our dreams than we sometimes do. Still, there are three things that really do put prayer images in a different category for me than dreams.

First, a dream, like an ordinary strong image in prayer, is not understood all at once. Rather, the experience of the dream or the image that comes up from our half-conscious mind is only the beginning of a great deal of interpretive psychological and theological work that must follow. For me, when a prayer image comes, however, there is no period of puzzling out its message. The prayer image speaks to the heart so immediately and so truthfully that there can be no mistaking its meaning. Furthermore, it will not only contain the clear solution to the problem I've been wrestling with; it will carry with it all sorts of saving insights into the ways the issue that has been gripping me has shaped the narrative of my whole life.

Second, unlike almost all dreams, when the prayer image comes in this way, it is so powerful that it almost appears to re-wire the brain. As you know, under ordinary circumstances, assimilating a new insight seems to be a slow process during which we come upon the insight, consider it, forget it, then rediscover it a few times—or even a few years—before it finally takes hold to replace what was there before. For me, prayer images don't work that way at all. There is none of the wavering back and forth between the old and the new. What is once learned by the heart through a prayer image is learned for good.

Third, even the most revelatory dream always seems basically to be from myself, the result of my dreaming dragging stuff up from my own unconscious mind. When I wake up from the dream, my emotional state is appropriate to the content of the dream: if I have dreamt of murder, I am afraid; if of anger, I am angry; if the situation I dreamt of was ambiguous, my feelings are full of ambiguity. The prayer image, however, is different. Whatever the content, whatever humiliating insight is there for me, whatever grief I meet with face to face, whatever of my own failing, the primary emotion I feel is not humiliation, grief, or shame. Rather, the new knowledge I have been given without fail is always carried on an overwhelming joy.

A significant part of this joy, I suppose, is predictable: I have been visited with the knowledge that this day salvation has come to my house. Still, this does not account for most of it, for the character of this joy is like nothing else I have experienced except, perhaps, being in love. The origin of the joy, I think, may have nothing to do with knowledge or healing at all. Rather, it comes from having found myself in the very presence of the God of love, the God in whose presence truth and goodness and beauty coincide, sweeping up everything into God's own self, which overflows with joy.

My friend, in my concern that you not misunderstand them, I don't want to underestimate the importance of these prayer images for me over the years. How incredibly grateful I am for them, both for the healing they have brought me, and for the presence of God who has brought them! Still, they carry with them their own problems. I freely admit to you that when they first came to me the temptation to think that they were somehow the point of all my prayer, or God forbid, even the reward of that prayer, was almost more than I could avoid. How could anything so overwhelming not be more real and more true than everyday prayer?

Yet over and over again, my teachers from the early church warned me: in the face of such an experience of God it is easy to prefer the powerful memory of the image to ordinary, everyday, routine prayer, even though it is in ordinary prayer that we live out our long-term, sustained, incarnational relationship with God. Nothing can be more real or more precious than ordinary prayer. This is why, I suspect, even from the beginning I had an instinctive conviction that my early monastic teachers were right to tell me to be grateful for the help prayer images gave me, but at the same time never to seek them out or ask for them.

There is one more thing you asked, my friend, and that is why some people have these images and others don't. That they are a gift of God I am in no doubt. Equally, I am absolutely certain that they do not come as a result of some special holiness or goodness or even special insight on the part of their receivers. So why some people, then, and not others? I'm afraid I just don't know. In my case, I have sometimes suspected, it is because I am often too dim or too hard of heart or too wounded to be able to learn any other way. Dear friend, please don't be afraid for yourself. God always finds ways to carry grace to our hearts if it is what we want. If you can't believe this about God, can you trust that I wouldn't tell you anything other than what I know to be true myself?

But a little while ago I promised to tell you about some of the work in prayer I have been doing over the past year that hasn't involved prayer images at all. Prayer images come as an unexpected gift, but if we pay attention, sometimes, because we are made in the image of God, what we need most comes up out of our own bodies. This is where a lot of the prayer of my ordinary time has lately been taking place.

Here is the way it started. On the first day of May this past year I went to see our family doctor. Three weeks before, at my annual visit, my gynecologist had done a blood test. Two or three days later she had phoned me at home to tell me that the part of the test results that covered cholesterol had come back high. She insisted that I go to my regular doctor and have it checked out. Her call frightened me and made me feel fatalistic. Heart disease is rampant in our family on my mother's side, and in the preceding months I had not felt well most of the time. I was glad, therefore, to have an excuse to try to make an appointment with my doctor. What I had not been glad about was his receptionist's non-negotiable insistence, first, that I repeat the blood test, which was to be done only at the end of an overnight fast, and second, that I could not see the doctor until at least ten-thirty later in the same morning. I did not fast well at all.

Sure enough, on the day of my appointment everything went just as I had expected. I arrived at nine o'clock for the blood work, my hands shaking, my head hurting, and shivering with nausea. During the following two hours of waiting my symptoms got worse. By eleven o'clock, when the doctor finally opened the door to the little cubicle, I was lying on the high, paper-covered table, half-naked and wholly sick. After greeting me politely he began at once to explain to me what he intended me to do about my cholesterol problem. As mentally confused as I was by now, however, I could hardly understand what he was saying to me, much less ask him questions of my own.

Still, I knew what my doctor was saying was important, and I like him besides, so I did the best I could to rally myself. I tried to answer his questions and to pay attention to his instructions and warnings about the medicine I was to take. I drew a deep breath of relief when the conversation appeared to be over. Finally, as he stood with his back half turned to me and his hand on the doorknob to go out, he asked me one last time if I had any questions of my own. "None that I can think of right now," I said, mumbling. Then, from nowhere my sense of shame fled and my self-preservation rose up in its place. "Oh yes, there is something," I said. "Is there anything in your office I could have to eat? I am not actually sure I can drive home right now, feeling the way I do."

At this last statement, the doctor's clean hand dropped off the doorknob. He turned back to the room and sat down on a stool by the door. I could feel him watching me closely as he questioned me and I answered him. What did I mean, that I couldn't drive home? How exactly did I feel? How long had I felt that way? Did I always feel like this when I hadn't eaten? How did I feel when I ate meat or didn't eat meat, when I ate a lot of carbohydrates or didn't eat many? What about coffee and alcohol? What about my sleeping?

A little later, he had made a diagnosis. I had a fairly common insulin-related blood condition that required me, if I wanted to begin to feel good and be able to think, to eat frequently, not to eat too many carbohydrates, to make sure I got enough protein, and to avoid sugar, alcohol, and caffeine. As I was shakily dressing, the nurse delivered a neatly made up paper plate of peanut butter and crackers and my new diet for hypoglycemia.

I remember that I left the doctor's office late that morning still mentally confused (peanut butter or no, it takes more than ten minutes for most snacks to make it from the stomach to the brain) but relieved and nearly euphoric. I didn't have heart disease or cancer or, much worse, hypochondria and terminal laziness. I knew now why I had been feeling so bad and so tired for so long, and I could do something about it simply by changing my eating patterns and what I ate.

In a burst of resolve and enthusiasm, I drove home carefully, ate, and went off to the grocery story in search of high-protein, low-carbohydrate, low-fat snacks, including a large supply of my favorite nearly fat-free hot dogs. Richard came home later. We cooked a good supper together in keeping with my new diet, and I explained it all to him while we ate. After that, we cleaned up, engaged in our usual evening activities, and went to bed. The next morning, I was still full of resolve about my diet and still energized. For breakfast I substituted an egg-white omelet for my usual cereal, then I had my prayers and began to write.

Just as you have surely predicted by now, I faced my first trial two hours after breakfast. I had been writing for about an hour when all of a sudden my hypoglycemia hit and I was ravenous. (Did I tell you that with this stuff I go from not-hungry-at-all to beside-myself-hungry in five minutes?) At this point, I knew what to do next, and I had been prepared to do it for two hours.

According to my new diet and anybody else's common sense, I should have gotten up, gone into the kitchen, eaten a snack without a fuss, and gone back to work.

This is not, however, how it went. The first thing that happened was this. At the very moment when I recognized that I was hungry, I was overcome with panic, guilt, and shame. At the next moment, my own nagging voice started up inside me. Eat? I couldn't possibly need to eat; I had only eaten two hours ago. What kind of person was I that I didn't have enough self-control to make it till lunchtime? I never had thought of anybody but myself, had I? my scolding voice went on. What about all the people in the world who went to bed hungry every night? Who did I think I was that I should eat just because I felt a little hungry? And furthermore, didn't I know that as a woman I had to look good if anybody was going to respect me? Surely I knew I was heavy enough already without making it worse by eating more!

At this point, of course, I could simply have told the voice in my head that it was wrong and it should be quiet. I wanted to eat not because I was a greedy, selfish person; I needed to eat so that I could think and be healthy. That having been done, I would have gone into the kitchen and eaten. This is not, however, what I did. Instead, I listened to the voice and collapsed under its pressure. By eleven o'clock I was exhausted and mentally confused, but still I had enough wit left to recognize that what up till now I had thought was a simple mechanical problem with an obvious physical solution, in fact, was going to be more complicated than it had first appeared.

I ate my lunch at noon, wondering with a fierce wonder what concrete wall I was hitting in myself. I knew, of course, that I had rediscovered for myself the important fact that my inappropriately guilty conscience, being as wounded as the rest of me, would frequently guide me very poorly if it were left to itself.

The next morning I began what turned out to be more than a week's excruciating work while I tried to see the wall I had hit. I began by asking myself in the presence of God what I intended to be a simple, obvious question. Where had this voice in my head come from that was threatening me with failure as a decent human being if I ate at times when for reasons of health and happiness I was "supposed" to eat? After a few days of going back into my memories, an answer had come back. As I find more often than not, however, this answer was not as simple as my question, and only one part of it, the easy part, strictly had to do with food at all.

What first emerged clearly to me in my prayer was the beginning of my difficulty with hunger, for strictly speaking it wasn't actually food that was causing the problem but my inability to eat when I needed to. I had been a baby during the Second World War, and a small child after it. During those years, in keeping with the need for a disciplined nation, the medical profession had decided that loving mothers should pick up their babies, hungry or not, and feed them only every four hours. It was a moral issue and it was an issue of character; if the babies cried from hunger and panic for three of those hours, that was too bad. Painful as it was, many young mothers who loved their babies as mine had done had not dared risk "spoiling" their children by going against the doctors' advice.

Contemplating all this in my prayer helped me see that I had learned two lessons as a baby before I ever had learned the word *milk*. First, I found out that hungry babies who cry are bad babies, or, to put it another way, that being hungry is a moral issue. Second, I saw for myself that there wasn't, and ought not to be, any internal connection between being hungry and eating. Rather, the sooner I was able to ignore my own body and accept that it was not I who would decide whether I would eat, but rather my mother or my father, the better.

I am sure I shared these same lessons in 1941 and the years following with thousands of other babies just like me. As I grew into childhood, my continued learning took on a slant peculiar first to my own family and then to me. As for the peculiarities of my family, meals and matters of food provided my father with a primary arena in which to exercise his authority over us children, and eating in his presence was always an anxious business. Certainly, he agreed with the theories that had dominated my babyhood, namely that there should be little connection between a child's own natural hunger and when and what that same child ate. My brother and I were to eat when and what we were told. A dessert was a reward for a clean plate without arguing. Talking back, being disobedient, a bad grade, gagging on the fat from meat (my father was convinced that eating fat was a kind of test of character), or not being able to force down some other food that made us sick, all merited the humiliating punishment of sitting at the table without dessert while everyone else ate theirs.

None of this, I suppose, would have been so bad, however, if I hadn't had my own food-related cycle of peculiarities that I carefully hid from my parents. The cycle all through elementary school went like this. I was so unhappy, and so terrified that I would make bad grades and get in some truly unspeakable trouble for it at school and with my father, that I could hardly sleep. I would wake up every morning about five o'clock or earlier so hungry and anxious I was beside myself. Breakfast, however, was so far away that by the time I was allowed to eat I was too nauseated from hunger and fear to be able to eat. Then, I remember, I would go to school where I could pay attention and learn only until about nine-thirty, when the mental confusion of hunger would descend upon me. There would be no eating, however, until the morning was over. By lunchtime I would have to throw my lunch away uneaten, my hungry stomachache, my mental confusion, my guilt and fear having made it impossible to swallow. At last, I would return home beaten down and exhausted at the end of the day. Then, my mother, having reasonably assumed that I had been eating normally all day, would give me a snack—two cookies and a glass of milk or an apple—small enough that it wouldn't ruin my appetite for supper.

I recall so much better than I wish I did how hungry I would be by supper. Regularly, I knew, this open, out-of-control hunger, which she saw as greed, would bring my mother to despair. Partly, this was because she longed for me to be a lady. Ladies in her farm family in Kentucky were expected to be good cooks, but they were not supposed to be particularly interested in actual eating. Still, there was more to it than that. To her, my very appetite was a betrayal of everything she stood for into what she thought of as the despising hands of my city father's family. "Just look at you," she would say, as she reminded me one more time of the story of a homemade fudge cake my father's sister, my aunt, had eaten in one sitting. "You are just like your Auntie Ree."

Oh, my friend, how hard all this was around food in my childhood and how intimately, inextricably, interwoven it was with what I had begun discovering as a baby—that I must learn to ignore what my own body had to tell me and accept, instead, that the adults in my life would decide what it needed, what it ought to do, and what it ought to be! How much, by this time, I wanted to abandon the work of my prayer!

It seemed to me now, as I newly thought about it in this way, that a huge portion of what I had had to teach myself at first, if I were to be allowed to be, was physical inactivity. My parents and I lived with my grandmother when I was a baby; after that we were in a duplex and then, in my elementary school years, in another small apartment, none of which had much room for the normal movement of children. Certainly, my father wasn't about to tolerate mine, or my noise, either. It was an almost daily experience when I was small that within ten minutes of my father's return from work his voice would be raised in that particular authoritarian way he had, "I don't care what you say; I don't want to know it." "I told you once not to run in the house," he would say, "now you go and sit in your room and be quiet until I tell you you can come out."

I am not sure how old I was when both my parents, but especially my mother, began to add an extra element to what they were telling me about my body. I remember one particular event that took place at home on a rainy weekend in the fall when I was about seven. I had been lying reading, sprawled in the living room, one leg up over the end of the couch while my parents took their Sunday afternoon nap in their room. I had heard my father moving around in the bathroom, but I hadn't been prepared when he had come into the living room. I glanced up from my book just in time to see him look at me, his mouth drawn straight with anger and disgust.

"Look at you!" he said to me. "Mary," he called my mother from the bedroom, "come in here and look at your daughter." I remember blushing hotly and looking down at myself in shame and fear. What had I done wrong this time just by lying there reading that had provoked my father so?

By then my mother had rushed in. "Just look at your daughter," he said to her. "For God's sake, teach her something!" Embarrassed by his implied criticism of her as well as me, my mother saw what he had seen. "For heaven's sake," she said to me, her own voice full of anger and shame, "pull down that dress and sit up. Can't you ever learn to act like a lady? If you can't learn, there's no telling what will happen to you!"

Until this moment, I had been baffled by the nature of my crime. Now I was completely bewildered. It was true that the dress I was wearing was up around my waist (apart from winter leggings, there were no such things as pants or jeans for little girls in those days), but what was so terrible about that? What had I done to make my parents go from restricting my bodily move-ment to finding something shameful and dangerous even in the manner of my physical inactivity? I couldn't dare ask, but I could see without asking that the danger that lay in wait for me if I didn't learn to take my body in hand extended far beyond the borders of my family.

As I had been trying to learn to be good by ignoring what my body was telling me about my hunger for food, so now I tried to teach myself to be good by making my body as small, unthreatening, and immovable as I could make it. Still, I remember quite clearly that I could never really understand what the offense of my body was that made this necessary, or whether there was anything I could do about it. My mother would get fed up with my reading in the house after school and send me against my will outside to play. There I could see for myself that there was a connection between my parents' unexplained instructions and the way the tougher boys, playing cowboys and Indians, would taunt me and twist my arm, run to the back of the apartment complex and leave me tied to a tree, my arms pinned to my sides. It was because I had the body of a girl, a contemptible body that was contemptible precisely because it was not permitted that girls should move their bodies freely or actively defend themselves from attack.

"But, Roberta, how did you deal with all of this about food and about your body?" I can hear you asking me now. "Surely, you didn't simply knuckle under and accept it, did you?"

I'm sorry to tell you that, throughout the rest of my elementary years, for the most part I did. Oh, I sneaked candy when I could, but it was hardly an act of defiance. One Christmas my step-grandmother gave my mother a ten-pound box of chocolates, and I would steal a few pieces nearly every day during the weeks she left it on the buffet. Their smooth texture lingers in my mouth even now and the way they soothed my sore stomach, but my guilt was so great that the theft was hardly worth it.

I did have my fantasies of perfectly free movement and they were very strong. There were times when I would dream almost every night that I had discovered how, just by breathing in a special way and flexing my muscles, I could take off into the air and fly. In those nights I would soar with perfect freedom and happiness over grass and animals and people. I still remember the wonderful way my legs would tense and jump up, smooth and powerful. I think the only time in my childhood I ever really felt my muscles positively was in these flying dreams. Though I did not have them so frequently in my adult life, certainly, these flying dreams continued well into my forties.

All my fantasies were not nocturnal, however. I recall one autumn that a man came from a local dancing school to recruit girls for ballet classes. He talked to my mother. My mother was interested; I was beside myself with excitement. In the two or three days before my mother brought it up with my father, who, of course, forbade it, I imagined continually the sensation of leaping without effort, of turning on my toes so quickly that my body was a blur, of stretching out my bent-over body and extending my head and neck as far as the sky.

Still, none of this was the daily reality. The negative stuff I've told you about my body and my own perception of it and my need to be "ladylike" only got worse and worse throughout my childhood. It peaked, I think, in Mrs. Evans's sixth-grade class, the year before my parents' divorce. There, I would shake so hard when she or George Whitefield, the meanest boy in the room, would even look at me that I would drop my pencil on the floor and send it rolling irretrievably under the radiator.

After that year, my parents were divorced, and because my mother didn't worry as much about clean plates or the character-building necessity of children swallowing down what was loathsome, this took the pressure off eating during family mealtimes. Furthermore, throughout junior high and high school, though I ate what turned out to be the things that actually aggravated what I now know was my hypoglycemia, I was not as panicked by the threat that I would not have food when I needed it because my snacks were no longer supervised.

This doesn't mean, however, that my food problems went away. My mother had been reared by a farmer father who sometimes had to leave the dinner table because he was so disgusted by the sound of his family chewing, and she was still convinced in her gut that ladies must display only minimal, unanimal-like interest in what they were eating. It was hardly surprising, then, that it seemed to me in those years that she was worried more than ever by my never-satisfied appetite, especially for sweets. By the time I was twelve years old, I had been caught up in the great American obsession with women's weight, women's clothes, and women's bodies, and I was repulsed and shamed by my ubiquitous hunger, myself.

Now, in my adolescent years, a new element was added to this mix of stuff about my eating and my body. Divorced and without the man people of the fifties thought every woman needed in order to survive, my mother spent her days, her nights, her brain, and her muscle straining and sweating to support and make a home for us children. Afraid for me and my own possibly manless future, she urged me daily to lay aside my physical inactivity; now I needed to stop being so lazy and learn to work hard.

In those years, her urging was only partly successful. I got a job selling costume jewelry at Grant's as soon as I was old enough. Other than that, there was nothing I could do. I was exhausted by my depression that never lifted and my hypoglycemic hunger that daily left me mentally confused and physically weak. Besides, by now, supported on all sides by the culture of the fifties, my earlier childhood lessons about femininity had taken on a life of their own. I was mesmerized by magazine articles by male psychologists who pronounced that women's happiness depended upon their ability to let themselves be passive receptors of male activity. I was enthralled by the images in those same magazines of helpless, feminine women, of light-bodied, long-haired ladies, cleaning the toilet in their high heels or fainting backward into the arms of handsome men. Whether or not my future happiness depended on believing all of this, I knew my social acceptance would. Certainly, I needed to believe it if I were not to hate my father.

It was all so expensive, and the coin in which I paid to believe it was so different from the promised currency of fulfillment. Once, walking down Bardstown Road in my baggy pants and flannel shirt, I was humiliated by a carload of boys leaning out the windows of their two-toned Bel Air Chevrolet, honking at me and whistling hog calls. Long since, my body had forgotten how to walk or move its arms or sit without self-consciousness. I had wanted to be invisible, to control its every damning movement, to become as unmoving, as above reproach as a stone. After that, I remember, I discovered that even breathing no longer seemed natural.

Oh, my friend, how hard it was that first week after the diagnosis of hypoglycemia, to relive and sort through in my prayer all these things of my childhood! By comparison, the next few days before I began to figure out how to deal with all of this were almost easy. This was the time in which I squinted and peered to see through the double lens of food and body what had happened to me in my adult life.

It was not as hard as I would have thought, for example, to recall how in my first marriage during my years in college, seminary, and graduate school, if I waited too long to cook supper, I would be almost too weak with hunger to stand up to do it. It was excruciating, however, to remember that, rather than finding a solution to it in the form of snacking or eating earlier, my husband and I both interpreted it as a sign of my lazy irresponsibility. I had puzzled often enough already how daily in graduate school I had become unable to think from the middle of the morning through the late afternoon, and how I believed that it was because I was mentally retarded or perhaps mentally ill. It still hurt, also, to recall the night in my first year at Oxford when a girl friend had teased me for my jerky, awkward movements once I had gotten brave enough at a Beatles party to try to dance.

As the days passed, sitting to pray in my red chair, I remembered with something like detachment the early years of my teaching before my dissertation was completed and after Grace was born. At that time, my own future survival depended upon my ability to ignore my body's messages of exhaustion, and so I had put to good use my mother's teaching about the need for women with families to learn to work until they dropped. Hypoglycemic and depressed as I was, I had to work without rest or help, not just on my academic work but also in the household. I recalled without too much distress what it had felt like for three years never to get a night's sleep that wasn't interrupted at least twice. What was still unbearably painful to remember was how more people than my husband had considered not only a wife's body but all of its energy as well to be the undisputed property of her husband, so that whatever teaching and research I did in those last years of the marriage was regarded as a kind of laziness and failure to do my duty as a wife.

Then, my friend, for a time the work became harder as I recalled, after that, the early years of my teaching. It was not easy to escape the pain of my own double conviction, shared by many other academic women and men of the seventies, that I could only hope to be taken seriously as a female scholar if I made myself sexually attractive to my male colleagues. I remembered what it felt like to know myself to be helpless in the simultaneous knowledge that these colleagues might well decide at any time to use that same sexual attractiveness as a reason to discount what I as a woman had to say.

Still, everything I remembered in that time was not all bad, and some of it was just what I would need to get me through the work that was coming up next. I thought of being pregnant with Anna Grace and Benjamin and how mysteriously strong I had discovered my body to be while I was giving birth. I experienced my pleasure again as I saw in my mind their little round nursing heads and I felt again my pride that I was able to feed another human being with milk from my own body. It was the only time in my life I could remember feeling proud of my body, friendly toward it, and shameless about it, and it helped me to remember.

Such good memories led me at last in my prayer to consider my actual present. The painful circumstances of my academic past in another place were gone. I was blessedly remarried, body and soul, to Richard. A few years ago, I had decided to try to reclaim my own body as best I could, and that was good. Because I wanted it to have substance, I did not want it judged as a woman's body in the old way, and because I no longer accepted that I must be hungry all the time, I had decided to eat pretty much what I wanted.

All this was good, too, but it had not solved the problems now before me, nor had it broken down the wall of enmity between myself and my own flesh. I had eaten what I wanted and I had gained substance by gaining weight, but I had not wanted the things that made me healthy or satisfied my appetite or made me strong. Furthermore, in spite of all my other gains, I still did not know how to swing my arms naturally when I walked or squat to pick up a book off the floor without jerky stiffness and embarrassment.

After a hard ten days, I had come at last to the end of digging around in and evaluating my past and present. I had discovered what I needed to know about the problems I was up against in myself in order to take them on in my prayer. The most immediate of these had to do with the hypoglycemia. I had to learn how to let my body be hungry without panic and shame, then eat the right things to satisfy it. Interwoven with the problem of my appetite, however, was the larger problem of my general relationship to my own flesh. Here it seemed to me that my task was to learn to pay attention to what my body was saying to me in the first place, in the hope that I might discover how to be truly incarnate, flesh and blood in it.

How was I to come at these two problems in my prayer and outside of it? The answer to the first of them seemed fairly straightforward and painless. I would read up on hypoglycemia to find out what foods were thought to be hurtful or helpful, in what combinations and at what times of day. I would learn to recognize the physical signals my body was giving me before I got desperate with hunger. Then, rather than panicking, trying to master my hunger by telling myself it was illegitimate, and then collapsing mentally and physically, I would simply have to go against my false conscience and force myself to eat. All this would be in the hope that, as the author of the fifth-century Macarian homilies used to say in reference to the development of the virtues, what would begin as a painful effort of the will would with practice first become a habit and then, at last, nature. As foundation for all this work, I would, with the grace of God, use part of my prayer time every day to find and draw on whatever images in scripture I could find to support my prayer. At the same time, every day I would pray the words of the Lord's Prayer, "give us this day our daily bread," with special care and attention.

My solution to the second problem, which was learning to live as an embodied human being, was more radical. For the time being, I was going to have to give up the basic form of prayer I had developed for myself over the years. It had stood me in good stead in the past and had brought me life spiritually and psychologically. Still, with its basis in quiet meditation, it depended on a physical passivity that was not what I needed now for the healing of the split between my body and the rest of me. What I did need was to work out for myself a new way of praying that would combine the physical, the spiritual, and the mental, the soul and the body into one.

Oh, my friend, how easy this was to decide to do and how scary in its implementation! How was I to give up what I knew? My prayer as I had learned it from my ancient teachers over the years had provided the solid foundation of my life; it had been my comfort, my thorn in the flesh, and my source of healing. Just as important, after my lifelong training in distrusting my body and being humiliated by it, how was I going to entrust it now with my prayer?

Two things, however, enabled me to go ahead with what I had decided. First, there was Richard and his experience. Three years previously Richard had found himself in a crisis. He was already anxious about some decisions he was making around a change in the direction in his career; on top of that, Benjamin was going off to college. From the time we had married, Richard had devoted his love and his energy to the children; and Benjamin, especially, the younger of the two, had given his stepfather a sense of himself and his own solidity on the earth. Now that part of Richard's life was over.

After mulling over the connection between his vocational anxiety and his loss of the role of parent as he had known it, Richard began to feel that what connected those things was something he described as a sense of weightlessness, of somehow being out of contact with the ground physically and psychologically, and he decided that what he had to do for himself was to begin to lift weights, to take on the spirit through the body. I am sorry to report to you, my friend, that at the time, I had been skeptical, to say the least, but Richard had very quickly proved me wrong. The physical effort and coordination it took to move and stress his muscles had been exactly what he needed to ground him in a new way in himself, the world, and God. For this reason, Richard, in his gentle way, was able to encourage me now to take the risk, to try something like it for myself.

Ironically, the other thing that made it possible for me to leave off praying in the way the ancient monks had taught me was a closer consideration of the prayer of the monks themselves. From the beginning, as I had seen it in the Life of St. Anthony (who was credited with being the first of the Egyptian monastic teachers[2]), one of the major goals of their prayer had been the restoration and health of the image of God within them. In the past I had found their teaching on the repair of the spiritual and psychological components of the image of God to be infinitely helpful to me. Still, coming as I did from my own set of body-soul–dividing twentieth-century prejudices, the often alien and sometimes bizarre nature of their ascetical practices had obscured for me the fact that they thought of their bodies as an important part of the image of God that was in need of repair as well. For this reason I had missed what they could have taught me about my own prayer and my body.

---

2. In the Life of St. Anthony, Athanasius describes Anthony coming out at the end of a many-year period of ascetical discipline in an abandoned fortress in the desert "neither too fat nor too thin," in perfect physical health as well as psychological health, like Adam before the fall.

Now for the first time I could hear my old and trustworthy teachers telling me that I *was* my body as well as my heart and mind, and that I should leave nothing of myself out of my prayer. I could adopt their general goal of the restoration of the body without their methods, which really were often self-defeating. I would not have to adopt their habit of praying standing up with my arms stretched out, for example, but I could find a way to pray that included the use of my arms and legs. I would not need to bend double at the waist more than a thousand times a day as one saint did when he prayed,[3] but I could develop my own way of bending and stretching and exerting physical energy in my prayer.

"We have never failed you before," they were urging me now; "take the risk and experiment," and so I did. During the second half of May, I began and ended my prayer as I always had with blessing my body by making on it the ancient sign of the cross. Then, I would tell God that I wanted to learn to live in and listen to the body God had given me and that I needed God's help to do it. After that, first for ten minutes and then for fifteen at a time, in the presence of God I rode the exercise bike that Richard had bought me, and that was my prayer.

After two weeks, having gained a little confidence and a little physical strength, I was ready to add some-

---

3. See the Life of Daniel the Stylite.

thing else to the daily ride on the exercise bike. I asked Richard to show me how to do a push-up, how to do a squat, and how to do a crunch, which is the modern equivalent of what in school we used to call a sit-up. Under the firm counsel of my monastic teachers, who always warned their disciples of the importance of thinking small if they intended to be able to keep up what they started, I began by doing only one of each, and I took a long period of lying on the floor between them.

As for these new exercises, they were much harder than the exercise bike. My arms would wobble and hurt and my neck and the tops of my shoulders would burn as though a torch were being held to them as I pushed myself up off the floor. The backs of my legs would pull and I would nearly lose my balance as I tried to squat and stand again, and on the crunch I barely had enough stomach muscles to get myself even once into its half-sitting position. It was hard work, and through it all not one single thing about the way I needed to hold myself, or breathe, or move my body felt natural.

This wasn't the only thing that made the work hard in the beginning. Predictably enough, the hard time I had learning to do these new exercises brought up all my old fears and shame and panic over my body, and it dragged up many otherwise forgotten memories as well.

Lying on the floor between my, by now, two push-ups and two crunches, for example, I remembered the first time in the second grade the teacher had taken my class to the gym. It had been to give us a fitness test. The test had only one component: We were each to do five squats and be graded on how well we did. I had been beside myself with terror over the idea of all the other children as well as the teacher watching me. When my turn came, dry-mouthed and sweaty-handed, I had pushed down blindly on my legs, and everyone except the teacher had laughed and hooted. My knees had, ignominiously, gone in instead of out, and I was in trouble again in school.

Still, little of this time on the floor between exercises was spent simply passively reliving the memories my muscles were squeezing out of my body. Rather, most of it was spent slowly, and sometimes furiously, bringing my memories and my body feelings into chaotic and extravagantly fruitful conversation with the images and stories from the scripture I had been so long accustomed to praying every day, sayings from my early monastic teachers, and the theological teachings from the early church that I had taught so long.

Let me give you an example of how all this worked. One day when I was beginning to despair that I would ever learn to breathe in and breathe out at the right times to be able to do the crunches correctly, I remembered recalling an embarrassing adolescent flute lesson when

I had been so unable to breathe correctly, my teacher had made me lie on my back on the floor and try it. I still hadn't been able to lose my self-consciousness enough to do it to my teacher's satisfaction.

Now, in the context of my place on the floor, it seemed to me that, just as I had never in my life moved naturally, neither had I ever felt as though it were all right for me to breathe deeply or naturally. Then, all at once everything I needed to help me out—memories, thoughts, feeling, theology—was there present in my mind. I remembered how, studying the notion of the "Spirit of God" that brooded over the waters of creation in Genesis chapter one, one of the first things I had learned was that the word for "wind," the word for "breath," and the word for "spirit" are the same. Next, my mind jumped forward in time to a more recent flute lesson in which my flute teacher had tried again to teach me how to breathe deeply. Finally, I remembered Jesus' promise to send his Spirit after his death, and I considered the meaning for me of the great wind that filled the room and swept over the disciples at Pentecost.

For two minutes more I lay there with all these pieces together in my mind, and at the end of them, I knew in my heart what everybody else seemed to have known all along—if the very scriptures describe God's Spirit in terms of breath, of wind, and of air, then it is good for me to breathe it. Two days after that, when I went to do a crunch, I found first my throat, and then my chest, and finally even the very lowest part of my abdomen where it had never been before, filling up wonderfully with air. And that breath of God, rejoicing every muscle as it went, smoothly lifted up my body, laid it down again, and began to root it solidly in the ground on which it lay.

This, my friend, is the way it has continued to go most of the time from then until now. Slowly I have lengthened the time I spend daily on the exercise bike to forty minutes a day, and I have found that I can combine riding with my earlier form of prayer that is basically meditation on scripture and a kind of centering prayer.

I have also gradually increased the number of daily stretching exercises that I do, and the number of times I do them. Twice a week I spend an extra fifteen minutes lifting weights, and it is wonderful to me each time to be aware of my back muscles and my leg muscles flexing and growing strong, to breathe deeply in rhythm with the tensing and straining of my arms and shoulders. After such a long separation from my body even my copious sweating feels good.

Always, every day, I end by lying on my back on the floor and praying the Lord's Prayer as I told you I had learned to do in my last letter. How continuously full of help it has remained for me as I have reflected on it in this process! Even now, each day as I continue to pay attention, to fight my panic, and to eat when I need to, its words stay with me. "Give us this day our daily bread"—give us today, the child I was and the adult I am, the basic food we need to thrive. Even now, I need to pray "thy kingdom come, thy will be done" in order that I not confuse the skimpy world my false conscience tells me God wants for me with the extravagant goodness of God's kingdom. Now, too, if I let myself, I am supported and encouraged by its closing words to recognize that God has the power, and has been exercising the power, to draw me into that kingdom and show me God's glory, "for the kingdom and the power and glory" really do belong to God, who shares them and shows them.

That my body really has begun to grow strong and that I am increasingly able to move and lift and push against and bend and squat with strength and confidence truly seems to me to be a miracle of the kingdom.

Even more of a miracle is this: my whole life the combination of the food stuff and the body stuff I've told you about has acted on me in such a way that I have believed that I could exercise no control over my body and its needs. This experience has somehow carried over to the rest of me in such a way that both in school and in personal relationships I have often felt helpless even in situations in which, if I could have brought myself to act or to speak up, I wouldn't have had to be helpless at all. Now, I am finding that by this process of combining my exercise and my prayer, as I am increasingly able to exert effort and move my body, this psychological sense of helplessness is leaving as well.

Nevertheless, my friend, in spite of all this good that is happening, I would not want to give you the impression that everything has gone smoothly all along, or for that matter, that I expect it to go smoothly in the future. I am, after all, doing the work of prayer here. Certainly, I have found that it is harder than I would have thought to continue to pay attention to what my body tries to tell me.

I had a period in September, for example, where I nearly lost everything. Coming off the summer, I have always had to push myself to my limits physically and emotionally the first month of school, and this year, without thinking about it, I expected this stress again as part of the job. Within a week I discovered that my exercise and new diet had given me ten times the energy I usually have in the fall. The old ways of "work till I drop" were no longer necessary. Rather than celebrating this fact, however, without even seeing what I was doing, I quickly moved this work mode from one part of my life to another. I decided that every day of the four or five days a week I was lifting weights I would increase what I lifted by a little bit until I could know that I was progressing as fast as I was able.

Of course, I did what any fool who knew me would know I would do. Every day I pushed myself to do more, all the while telling myself that I would stop when I hit my limits. The trouble was, I had made this decision on the basis of what I believed my body ought to do, rather than on the basis of what I had been trying to learn to do, namely, listen to it. Now, working out of theory rather than listening to my body, I couldn't tell when I had hit my limits. Within four weeks I was so exhausted at the end of my exercise that I could hardly make it up the stairs to my office. In bed at night, I slept like the dead. Still, I didn't connect my exhaustion with the exercise I was doing; I had moved too far back into the old familiar category of "ought" to hear the "this is what you are doing" my body was saying to me.

Then one day I realized I was physically feeling at least as bad as I had felt when the children were babies. I asked Richard whether he thought that I was sick, or whether he could think of anything else that was wrong. Needless to say, he had already had his ideas. Now, he looked over the charts I had only recently begun to keep (working out of my perpetual perception of myself as lazy, I had not thought the paltry weight I was lifting before then really merited recording). He was appalled and he told me why. Even so, it took him four solid days of gentle and not so gentle arguing to convince me that under the guise of progressing, I had gone right back psychologically to where I had started in May. Daily I was lifting many times the weight my body could tolerate without damage.

At last, reluctantly and going against my feeling and the promptings of my conscience that had continued through all this to tell me I was being lazy, I decided to accept Richard's judgment. He had carefully studied a number of books on exercising and weights for people who are over forty. I accepted it as well as I could, therefore, when he worked out what even now I am sometimes tempted to think of as the slacker's exercise program I follow in the present. My energy has gradually returned, and as I end my exercises each time I am increasingly aware of more small progress in my muscle and movement. That I learn to accept the slowness fully is part of the drudging, ongoing work of my prayer.

Still, backsliding or not, I know that I am making progress. The night last week after I wrote you about my childhood fantasy of dancing, I had a dream confirming this for me. In the dream I was on a research leave with Richard in a university somewhere in Italy. There, I agreed to baby-sit for the afternoon with the two-year-old daughter of a woman I knew. Soon after, smiling and friendly, the child arrived at our apartment dressed in a little pink and white organdy party dress of the forties, tiny patent leather shoes, and lace-edged socks. Because I was concerned that there was nothing for her to do in the apartment, I decided I would take her hand and let her lead me on a walk.

Next, the scene in the dream shifted to the inside of an ornate, many-pillared church to which she had led me. Now, however, she no longer held my hand. Instead, she was running ahead of me through a crowd of tourists toward an impressive yellow marble altar in the front on the left. As I tried to catch her I remember being terrified that the priest in charge would see us and throw us both out in disgrace.

This is not what happened, however. At the very moment the child ran up the steps to the altar a tall, serious-faced, gray-haired man in a clerical collar stepped out of the shadows and walked slowly down the steps toward her. As she held her arms up to him, he stooped down to pick her up; then he set her gently on the altar, saying, "Now you can dance!"

How those tiny feet in their fancy socks danced and how that pink and white dress whirled and swooped up there on that high altar, and how it made my heart lift to see it! When she had had enough, radiant and full of herself, she held out her arms for me to lift her back down. I squatted down next to her to hug her and smile at her. "You were dancing, babycakes," I said to her.

She clapped her hands and smiled herself; then she started to cry. "What's wrong?" I asked. "My mama's going to make me into a cake?" she said. I laughed and hugged her again. "No, that just means you're sweet," I replied. Once again she clapped her hands and laughed with me.

I cannot tell you precisely everything my dream was about. Upon reflection the next morning, however, I could identify two things the dream confirmed for me. First, in my new context of prayer and exercise, Jesus Christ, the great high priest himself, was enabling me to violate every taboo about my body I had ever learned. As a result, that unmoving child who had so longed to dance was dancing on the very altar of God.

Second, through all these months since I had first begun to pray the Lord's Prayer in the new way I told you about, I had continued to pray "may your name be made holy in the child I was, and may I myself see it." In this dream God's name was made holy in the body of that dancing child; I watched it happen with my own eyes. I am still watching and I am grateful.

My dear friend, I hope I have said something to make it a little easier for you to trust yourself and God and to believe in the ordinary processes of your own particular prayer. Know that you are held close in my heart.

With love,

*Roberta*

# FIVE

# The Yellow Shirt

*My dear friend,*

You are certainly right when you observed in your last letter that most of the wounds of the heart I write about have been those that have their origins in conditions or injuries we received in childhood. You are also right to notice that, when I talk about seeking the healing of those wounds, my emphasis mostly seems to fall on the kind of hard and deliberate work we ourselves need to do in prayer.

After puzzling over these two things a good while, you ended your letter with two really important questions. You wanted to know, first, if I believe that these wounds that have their origins in our individual past experience are the only significant kind of wounds that keep us from loving. Second, you asked if I really mean to suggest that healing comes to us in prayer only as a result of the kind of hard and deliberate work I have been talking about.

The answer to the first question is absolutely not. All of us have other kinds of wounds that need healing that keep us from loving just as effectively as wounds that have their origins in our individual childhood experience. Unlike the first kind of wounds, these other injuries to our ability to love and be loved have their origins more in attitudes and expectations that we have picked up and taken for granted from our culture, even our church culture, than our private, individual experience. So we come to look at the world and the people in it, dismissing some and valuing others not as God does, but as our own larger culture does.

When these moral wounds that have their origins in what we've learned from our larger culture are reinforced by the wounds of our personal experience, the results are often deadly, to ourselves and to others. Not surprisingly, these combination wounds are also in some ways the hardest to be healed of because we have so much at stake in not even seeing we have them. Even if we don't have any reason to keep from seeing them, how can we seek healing for what we don't even know is wrong?

The fact that we can't at first see them in order to work at them directly in our prayer does not mean, however, that God will necessarily abandon us to them. Do you remember some letters ago when I talked about the fact that all healing in prayer is the result of a combination of God's work and our own? Evagrius Ponticus, one of the greatest of the fourth-century monastic teachers, used to say that this is true also of prayer itself. "If you wish to pray," he would say, "then it is God whom you need. [God] it is who gives prayer to the [one] who prays."[1] It is my experience that in these situations in which we need healing but in our ignorance cannot help ourselves, it is God who comes to us with grace and help for healing.

As for our own part in this work, part of our job is simply to be there, always attentive to what we are doing and what is going on inside us, at the same time we listen and pay attention to the people and events around us. Part of our job is to expect that, if we are attentive and willing, God will "give us prayer," will give us the things we need, "our daily bread," to heal and grow in love.

But this is enough about theory. I think it will be more helpful if I tell you a story illustrating what I am talking about. It is the story of one of the most significant events

---

1. Evagrius Ponticus, Chapters on Prayer 58. *The Praktikos*, Chapters on Prayer, trans. John E. Bamberger, Cistercian Studies, 1970, p. 64.

I have ever lived through: the death and funeral of Stefan Mills, the child of my friends Nicole and John.

* * * * * * * * * * * * * * * * * * * * * * * * * * * * * * * * * * * * * * * * * * * * *

The beginning came for me at 7:30 one rainy gray Saturday morning toward the end of August with the ringing of the phone. I was on the exercise bike and halfway through my prayers. Under ordinary circumstances, I would not have stopped either my prayers or my exercise to answer the phone, but these were not ordinary circumstances.

Planning a detour to pay a visit in northern Indiana, Benjamin, our son, had driven off at the beginning of the preceding week to begin his senior year in college. Only the day before, on Friday, Richard had followed him up with a truckload of his things. He would help Ben get set up in the house he was to share with some classmates, then Richard would stop off on his way home to check on his brother in Cincinnati. Benjamin or Richard could still be on the road; one or both of them could have had an accident. Exercising or not, therefore, the very sound of the phone ringing had brought the blood to my head with a rush.

Certainly, loss was on my mind that morning. With his own characteristic mixture of enthusiasm and reluctance Benjamin had told us in June that this would be his last summer at home. Richard and I had spent the previous months getting used to the idea. We had been as matter of fact about it all as we could; we knew that children need to leave home to grow up. Prepared parents that we were, seeing him pack up his clothes, his schoolbooks, and his stereo as he had done every year before had not been too hard on us, and it hadn't seemed too hard for him, either.

In the end, however, when Benjamin took down the bed he had slept in since childhood, disassembled his desk, and carried them both out along with his dresser and his lamps and his teddy bear, it was too much for any of us. He had already spent his week of packing brooding on the end of the securities, such as they were, of his childhood and dreading the unknown terrors of adult life. He had stood in his empty room and cried like a baby.

I had cried with him. I had alternately grieved his going as though I would never see him again, and been angry that I should have to do this mourning all over again as though I'd never done it when he'd first gone to college. The afternoon he left, the sight of his old gray van turning into the road from the end of the driveway filled me with desolation.

In the few days that followed Ben's leaving, Richard and I had fought his going in our own characteristic ways. Possessed with the demon energy of grief and new beginnings, Richard had immediately taken forty-eight hours to clean the deserted room and fix it up as a combination bedroom for Ben's subsequent visits and as an exercise room for the two of us. For my part, I had moped around self-pityingly and thought black thoughts; then I had gone ahead and made plans to do pleasant and distracting things with friends during the upcoming weekend when Richard and Benjamin would both be gone.

One of these things that I had looked forward to that Saturday morning was going to an art show with my old friend Nicole. Nicole is my own age, a founding member of Emmaus, our house church community, and a lover of God. She is also a Frenchwoman, stylish, intelligent, and an artist who used to dye and weave her own fabrics. Now, with lupus and arthritis, her sore and swollen hands are only able on their good days to make beautiful earrings and necklaces. Nicole was the right person to go out with. Though she sometimes gets ground down with pain, she has a good spirit; she has a passionate interest in every person she meets, especially in children and young people, whom she treats exactly as she does her adult friends. Since the time my children were small they both have thought her wonderful.

At any rate, it was because of my planned outing later in the morning that I had tried to exercise some common sense when the phone rang. It was far more likely to be Nicole calling to change the time we were going or putting off our trip because of the rain than it was to be a report of something having happened to Richard or Benjamin.

Common sense or not, still, I let out the breath I had been holding when I picked up the phone and heard that it was only a very stuffed-up Nicole on the other end calling from a phone with a bad connection. It took me a moment or two to realize that she was trying, in a voice I didn't quite recognize, to explain something to me I couldn't quite catch.

I tried for a little while to puzzle out what she was saying, then I gave up. "Wait, Nicole," I interrupted her. "I can't understand you. Are you sick? Do you have a cold? Are you calling me to cancel our trip?" I asked. Then I added, "Don't worry; we can try again tomorrow morning if we need to."

"No, no, you don't understand," she got through to me at last. "It's Stefan; he's been hit on his motorcycle."

"Stefan?" I said. For a moment I was speechless. Stefan was her younger son; he was twenty-six years old, the same age exactly as our daughter, Grace. Though they hadn't really been friends, they had been in school together from the fourth grade to the middle of high school.

Nicole began to cry; my stomach turning over, I strained to take in what she was saying. "The doctor said he might be dying, and if he doesn't die, he'll probably be a vegetable," she said.

"It's Stefan?" My mind was lagging far behind what she was telling me. "Stefan had an accident? He might be dying?" I repeated, horrified with shock. "Oh, Nicole, poor Stefan," I blurted out at last. "Are you at DeKalb Hospital?"

"No," she was barely able to answer, "we are downtown at Grady, on the seventh floor."

"Grady?" I repeated blankly. "Stefan is at Grady? Does Betsy know?" I asked, trying to think. Nicole and John have an extraordinary number of friends, but Betsy and her daughter, Paula, are as old and dear to them as any in Atlanta. Betsy is a retired high school assistant principal with a sense of adventure and a desire to do good; she now spends her days traveling the world and giving workshops on all sorts of interesting things relating to conflict resolution. She is also one of the founding members of our house church, a definite and funny woman whose friendship and moral strength would be greatly needed in the time ahead.

"I already called Betsy," Nicole answered.

"All right, I'll be right down," I said. I could hear her crying as she hung up the phone.

Once off the phone, stricken with the knowledge of this disaster that had befallen our friends Nicole and John, I could only stand in the middle of the room, paralyzed with pain for them. Stefan, their son, was lying unconscious in Grady Hospital, and only an hour before I had been feeling sorry for myself that Benjamin, my own son, had simply left home to grow up.

When I could move at last, I called Terri, another of our close friends through Emmaus, and arranged to pick her up on my way downtown. I had a quick shower, praying like a crazy woman all the while, that God would keep Stefan close and comfort the hearts of Nicole and John. Then, for my hypoglycemia, I stuffed a handful of paper-thin crackers and a cold pork chop in a plastic bag into my pocketbook and went.

All the way to Terri's house I thought of our daughter, Grace, and of my own continuous anger and fear for her during the two years of her adolescence when she had ridden a succession of ever more powerful motor-cycles. That whole time, I had gone to bed every night expecting a phone call like the one that had summoned John and Nicole to the hospital. I had felt so relieved after the last bike was sold. Driving through the green light at Ponce de Leon and Highland Avenue, I wondered now why it should have been Nicole and John who received that call and not us.

A few moments later I picked up Terri. As we drove downtown we talked of Stefan and the mystery of his life, and the hard time he had had over the years; we talked of the desperation, the goodness, and the loyalty with which Nicole and John had loved him. We spoke of the two or three years of his teen years, when in spite of anything John and Nicole could think to do, he had lived almost on the streets with other young and not so young people, tattooed and pierced not just in body but in soul, too, it seemed to me, just like himself. We talked about his long stay in the mental hospital and how little it had helped him, and about the time since, in which he had lived still among his old friends at the edges of our own middle-class world, unsuccessfully trying to hold down a variety of jobs for short periods of time in hardware stores, florists, and an assortment of clubs, all the while riding the motorcycles he loved.

We spoke of the invariable politeness and friendliness with which he had always spoken to us when he had been staying with his parents, even when we woke him with early morning phone calls to the house. We talked about what we had heard our friends who had known him as a little child say of him over the years, how sweet he had been, how funny and how loving. And we wondered and wondered at the strange haplessness and innocence that had stayed with him from the times we had first known him right into the very present. After a while, we arrived at Grady.

Grady is a big and confusing hospital and trauma center; it took us nearly forty-five minutes to find our way from the place we parked on the street to the elevator on the seventh floor. Of those first moments in the hospital, I recall the anxiety we felt as we stumbled around the confusing corridors to locate the waiting room where our friends were. Equally, I recall the almost physical sense of relief we felt once we found them—Nicole and John, their elder son, Christopher, and Laurie, to whom he would become engaged on Monday night.

From the first hours of that morning, however, there are several things that now stand out in my mind which are much more significant than our anxiety and relief. Foremost among them is my memory of the presence and the general appearance of several women and men of various ages who were there in the hospital in connection with Stefan's accident. Some of them, I remember, drifted through the corridor that ran by the little lounge where we sat; some of them stood back, unspeaking in the shadows across from us like ghosts. They were the friends of Stefan, Nicole explained. They had met him at the bar after work the night before when he had been hit. They had also been quick to find Nicole and John after the accident and call them, and from what I heard, they had stayed close to them, attentive and gentle, until the rest of us began to arrive.

Still, what I remember now to my shame is that, whatever John and Nicole had to say about them, I wanted nothing to do with them. With their impassive faces, multiple earrings, eyebrow rings, large tattoos, spiky hair, black lipstick, big boots, and pale skin, I was frightened of them, and I disliked them. In those first hours, I couldn't understand why they, like Stefan himself, had chosen to live lives that seemed to me to be so chaotic, so brutal, and above all, so meaningless. I think I blamed them for what was happening to Stefan's whole family. Certainly, I wished that they would go away.

Simultaneous to this memory, I also remember waiting on the black plastic chairs of the little lounge for the neurosurgeon's report while John told us what had happened in the accident the night before. Hunched cold in her black jacket, Nicole cried and cried some more while John recounted the story.

At midnight after work Stefan had gone with some friends to a club downtown. He had known that he would be on his motorcycle, his friends were eager to say, and he had been careful not to drink. Around two o'clock in the morning some of them had left to go home. Not far out of the parking lot, Stefan had collided with an uninsured man from Alabama in a Lincoln Continental, coming out of a gas station. The police, who had seen the accident, immediately arrested the driver of the car. Stefan had been thrown in the air fifty-two feet; he had landed on his head on a concrete planter.

The friend who had seen the accident rushed to call an ambulance, and someone else located John and Nicole. Not much more than ten minutes after the accident Stefan was at Grady. Because of the speed of the impact and the distance he had traveled, his heavy motorcycle helmet had done him no good. He had suffered a broken collarbone, broken ribs, a punctured lung, a broken foot, and, most serious, a fractured skull.

After this account, shocked into silence, we hunched down to wait for the neurosurgeon who was attending Stefan. A long time passed. Several residents and nurses came to report to his parents what they were doing to him and for him, and to offer cautious hope for his recovery. Even at the time I was struck with gratitude by the kindness of those harassed people in that busy hospital and the care they took to listen to the family's questions and answer honestly.

The neurosurgeon arrived at last. Plainly, he was a good man, but he was awkward. Only after he had been talking in circles for a good long while did I realize that he was uncomfortable trying to find a kind way to speak the truth about the nature and seriousness of Stefan's head injuries. Finally, at the end of one interminable sentence, the doctor gave up and simply blurted out, "He's probably not going to make it, you know."

John and Nicole were unprepared for this in spite of what they had already known. John had sat as still as the green marble wall behind him, but Nicole had cried out, "What did you say? What did you say?" When the doctor repeated his words, she had bent double, shaking with sobs. In a moment John began to sob, too. Christopher had sat beside him, his eyes closed and his mouth clamped shut, unable to make a sound while the tears ran down his face. The doctor crept away, and Terri and I had put our arms around our friends, longing in vain to take some of this terrible pain off them by taking it into ourselves, instead.

I had been praying continuously for Stefan and his family ever since I had arrived at the hospital. Still, I think it was only at that moment of intense grief for Stefan and his family that I became fully conscious that what was happening in there in the hospital was as sacredly important as anything I had ever been a part of. Certainly, I was intensely aware of my gratitude that Nicole and John and Christopher should have let me stand there praying with them in that place where God is found, where life and death come together. I was aware, too, of the gratitude I felt to our gentle and mysterious God, who I knew, in spite of everything, was holding all of us in a profound sense of God's goodness and generous love.

I remember as part of all that, a strange sense of hyper-alertness, which was there not only in myself but that, as the day went on, I could see repeated both in the gathering faces of Stefan's family, and throughout the next days in the faces of the many other friends who came to the hospital to wait. When it was that I was able to call this super-alertness by its right name, I am not sure, but I know its name now. In Romans, Paul speaks of the Spirit searching our depths and praying in us, and this is what it was. It was prayer, pure and concentrated, an almost physical straining of our whole beings to pay absolute attention to what was happening, to God present with us, vibrating in our bellies and breastbones like the deep sound of bells. Yet, praying even so, there were things, important things, I myself should have understood but wouldn't even begin to understand until much more time would pass.

A little later, when the doctors and nurses had finally finished cleaning up Stefan and bandaging his injuries and he was hooked up to the many machines and dials and little dripping bags that would sustain his life for the next three days, I went for the first time to visit Stefan in the small intensive care room in which he died. I was shocked by his appearance. I had been prepared for Stefan's unconsciousness. What I was not prepared for was how big and muscular and healthy Stefan's torso looked in his high, metal-framed bed, and how beautiful his face was as he lay there in his terrible coma. I remember wondering at the smoothness of his skin and the fact that it was the exact same deep tan color as his mother's. It somehow shook my heart that he should have such a serious head injury, and yet have no marks on his face, so many broken parts, and so few visible bruises.

When I got back to the little lounge where I had left Nicole, Christopher, and Laurie, I found that the first round of Nicole and John's friends—and mine, too— had begun to arrive. Betsy had come while I was in

Stefan's room, bringing her courage and her matter-of-fact wisdom as well as a thermos of the hot water Nicole likes to drink, and cheese, fruit, and cake. A little later Betsy's housemate, Sheila, came, a person of no mean wisdom herself. After her, Mili and Fernando, some other old friends from Emmaus who had known all the Millses a long time arrived with some hot Puerto Rican coffee and another cake, and because Fernando is a physician with the Centers for Disease Control, a great deal of medical knowledge as well.

The next few hours among these friends were full of conversation, eating and drinking, crying and laughter. In spite of Nicole and John's grief and our excruciating anxiety about whether Stefan would live and if he did, how injured he would remain, the time was oddly full of God's goodness. Never before do I remember being so much of one heart, one mind, and especially one strength with people who so loved one another that the very language of the "body of Christ" ceased to be a metaphor and became, instead, a literal description of the way we were together. We leaned on one another to support our friends, but the strength with which we held one another and which upheld us all was not our own strength, but that of Christ's own self who lived within us binding us into one, as solid as the ground and deep as the core of the universe.

During those hours in that holy space we friends spoke of everything we had shared together, as well as of Stefan, his innocence, his troubles, and whether he would live. I remember that we found a lot that was funny. We told outrageous jokes and punned the bad puns John thrives on. Nicole laughed and laughed when I finally set my embarrassment aside and took my leftover cold pork chop out of my pocketbook for lunch. We laughed with her, and we affirmed our love with our laughter, the reality of life, and the goodness of God.

Surely, that laughter was sacred. Later, in the early afternoon, when I pulled out the packet of paper-thin crackers I had brought to supplement my pork chop, Sheila snatched one of them out of my hands and laughing, held it up for everyone to see. "Ridiculous!" she said over it as she began to break off little pieces of a cracker and pass them out among us. "The body of Christ," she said to me in parody, handing me a broken piece. Suddenly, tears rose in my eyes. Without warning, the little crumb of cracker really had become the body of Christ, and I knew, without any shadow hiding it, that the weight and glory and the laughter of the crucified and risen Christ was there among us blessing us.

It was soon after that, I think, that I was able to begin to take in a little the crowd of Stefan's friends who, from Saturday morning until the Monday night before he died, occupied the rainy outside steps of the hospital and filled the big lounge on the seventh floor. This, at least, was when I began to hear, to really hear, the stories

that Nicole and John repeated to us that Stefan's friends
were telling them about him.

Mostly, they were amazing stories of Stefan's kind-
nesses and the care he had taken of those who could not
help themselves. To me, the academic, the most striking
of these was the witness of a Ph.D. student in brain
chemistry who had frequently become demoralized and
ready to quit his work as he struggled with his dissertation. Stefan, who had never himself completed more
than his sophomore year in high school, had called this
scientist once a week over a long period of time to raise
his spirits by asking him the most detailed and intelligent
questions relating to what he was working on and what
he had been writing.

But this was only one testimony. There were many
others, like that of the woman who had driven directly
to the hospital all the way from Florida when she had
heard of Stefan's accident. Three years ago she had
moved all alone from Atlanta to Florida. She had become terribly depressed. Her, too, Stefan had called
frequently, to support her and comfort her in some
extraordinary way that had enabled her to keep on
going.

As John and Nicole reported these stories to us, I
understood that not only they, but we other middle-class
folk too, were being strengthened and comforted im-
measurably by what we were hearing. We were learning

about a Stefan who was much more extraordinarily deliberate and active in generous love, and his world much fuller of coherently good people than any of us, even his parents who knew and loved him best, had ever imagined. At the same time, we were beginning to experience for ourselves the unexpected goodness, generosity, and sensitivity of the community of people among whom Stefan had chosen to live.

Shortly before five o'clock I left, exhausted and anxious to prepare for the next day's faculty retreat that opens our school year. It was almost more than I could do to leave, but my presence really wasn't needed. As they had heard the news, John and Nicole's friends had continued to arrive all afternoon to share the vigil at the hospital, and others were already on their way. Among them were Elaine and Dale who, over the next few days, did more useful things, including entertaining John's parents, than anybody can ever imagine.

\* \* \* \* \* \* \* \* \* \* \* \* \* \* \* \* \* \* \* \* \* \* \* \* \* \* \* \* \* \* \* \* \* \* \* \* \* \* \* \* \*

It was hard to go to the retreat the next day. In the morning when I went to the hospital before I drove up to the state park where it was to be held, I found Nicole and John worn out and frantic with worry. Stefan was in the state Fernando had warned us to expect the night before: He had been alternating between periods of relative stability and periods of crisis of one sort or another that ranged from pressure in the brain to organ failure and high fever. The retreat was not to be over until Tuesday afternoon; I was worried Stefan would not live that long. How could I go away and leave them?

I went because we were told that Stefan could be in this condition for a very long time. Still, once there, I simply couldn't concentrate. I went to bed early Sunday night and woke early the next morning. Around eleven o'clock I left the meetings to talk first to Betsy, then to Nicole. Stefan was worse; the doctors were preparing to begin their very complicated tests to determine if Stefan were brain dead so that he could become an organ donor. At noon, I gave it up. I left the retreat with the dean's blessings, and drove the two hours back to Atlanta.

I arrived at the hospital in the middle of Monday afternoon to find things very different from what they'd been the morning before. The halls and little lounge were full of the anxious relatives of the victims of a plane crash in Alabama, and everyone there for Stefan had been moved into the enormous inside waiting room. There was only a handful of people there now, though many of the new visitors were folks from out of town. The visitors for John and Nicole huddled toward the right-hand wall, talking cursorily around a table of half-eaten food. A lone friend of Stefan's who had obviously been there all night was asleep on a couch in the middle of the big room, his leather jacket zipped to the neck and his crutches beside him. That night he told me that he was about to have an operation for a hip replacement. He himself had also had a motorcycle accident ten years before, and sadly he had explained how Stefan had been there to help him, too.

As for Nicole and John, many glitches during the day had prevented the doctors from running the tests they had planned for Stefan. Though his condition was deteriorating fast, neither of his parents had quite given up hope that their son would live. The little group of people there in that waiting room, but especially Nicole, looked exhausted and strung out.

After a few minutes in that long, now dreary room, I went to see Stefan in intensive care. As I walked in through the door, John was at the end of the bed, tears dripping off his nose as he rubbed Stefan's uninjured foot. He was too focused to pay much attention to new visitors. His eyes moved between the tall monitors to the left of the head of the bed and Stefan as he urged him, "Make that heart beat, son, keep that heart beating." As for Stefan himself, he was obviously failing. The nails of his hands were blue and his body had begun to look battered.

It was only after I had been there a while that I realized I was not the only visitor in the room. Not until he went through the door like a shadow did I realize that one of Stefan's friends had been there, too. Where he had been exactly, I am still not sure; perhaps in front of the chair under the window. Certainly, it was not until he left that I noticed the presence of a man's shirt draped back to front over the small wooden chair on the window side of the bed. John saw me looking at it. "It's Christopher's shirt," he said. "Stefan always admired it, and Stefan's friends went to Christopher's and got it, hoping it would help him."

The shirt was extravagantly gorgeous, the back of it covered with an exotic bird and little bunches of flowers and leaves in intense colors, cherry reds, electric blues, and emerald greens against a background of the brightest, sunniest yellow. It was beautiful, and in that terrible place of the machinery of life and death where Stefan lay, it seemed to me incongruous and a little jarring. Stefan was past help now; how on earth, I wondered half-bitterly to myself, could anyone think that such a shirt, such a gesture, would help Stefan?

Now, many weeks later, having chanced in my prayer on a parallel story from the gospels, it seems strange to me that at the time I could not understand what I was seeing.

The story as I came across it takes place at a banquet Mary, Martha, and Lazarus give for Jesus and the disciples at the beginning of Holy Week.[2] It is a dangerous time, and Mary, at least, knows that Jesus' life is at particular risk. Suddenly, Mary leaves the room where they are eating; she comes back with a whole pound of expensive perfume. Then, while the house fills with its

---

2. John 12:1-8. In the telling of the story in the other gospels, the woman is not Mary the sister of Martha.

wonderful smell, she pours the perfume over Jesus' feet and wipes them with her own long hair. "What is she doing?" The disciples, I suspect, stir with outrage. Shamelessly, Judas objects, "Wasteful, wasteful! What about the poor?"

Aware, it seems to me, that their reaction has nothing to do with the poor and everything to do with their sense that she has encroached upon their own privileged position, Jesus answers. "Leave her alone," he says. "Leave her alone; she bought it so that she might keep it for the day of my burial."

How much Jesus must have needed that perfume, the living proof that a person who loved him really understood the reality of what was happening to him and was prepared to stand there in it with him! Of course, the shirt brought by Stefan's friends was not quite like Mary's anointing of Jesus for his burial. The shirt, rather, was a gesture of last-minute hope for his recovery. Still, as Jesus was once strengthened by Mary's gift of perfume, so I am sure that Stefan must have been strengthened for what lay ahead of him by the presence in his room of that incredible, inappropriate shirt. How very sorry I am that I could not see it—that even as late as this, I was found, not among the perfume pourers with Mary, but with Judas among the despisers!

After my visit to Stefan I returned to the big room to wait with those who were there. As the afternoon lengthened, Betsy and I made numerous phone calls to the friends who needed news. Gradually, as the tension built toward five o'clock the big room began to fill again with the two sets of friends: Stefan's friends, silent and serious in one large corner, Nicole and John's friends spread out in the rest of the room, talking quietly as we waited. Around six o'clock Richard arrived from taking Ben to college and visiting his brother in Cincinnati. Almost immediately he went out with John to talk to Stefan's friends who were smoking on the front steps of the hospital.

Shortly after Richard and John returned to the waiting room the doctors summoned Nicole, John, and Christopher to Stefan's room to tell them they wouldn't be doing the tests. Stefan would die before the night was out, and except for his eyes all his organs were too deteriorated to be donated. That he couldn't be an organ donor was an unbearable blow to his parents.

It was at this terrible low point, when they didn't know what to do and we didn't know how to help them, that Nora, a Dominican chaplain at the hospital and a good friend both of the Millses' and of our community, went to Stefan's family in the intensive care unit. Blessedly, Nora knew what to do; she told the three of them to sit in the room with their son and brother, and, assuming that in some mysterious way he could hear them, tell him everything they felt he needed to know before he went—of their love, of their memories, of their sorrow and regrets. This, to their comfort, is what they did. One at a time some of us, I among them, went too, to say good-bye.

During this time Nicole and John came out periodically to talk to the visitors who continued to come to keep vigil. Jackie brought her adopted Chinese baby, Rose, and I remember the pleasure Nicole took in the smiling little girl who ran up to her to sit on her lap. Most of all, however, it was Stefan's friends, by now an amazing forty or fifty of them, who comforted and strengthened Nicole and John as they continued to come to them one by one to share their stories of Stefan, what he had done for them and what he had meant to them. We, the middle-class friends who filled our part of the waiting room, sat or stood in little talking clumps, sad and empty, too distracted now to think beyond the moment. In endurance mode, we continued to wait.

Then, around ten o'clock something happened. Some of Stefan's worn-out, battered-looking friends approached Betsy's housemate, Sheila. Many of us belonged to John and Nicole's church, they said to her, and they knew we were religious people. Would one of us be willing to lead them in a prayer service for Stefan?

Would one of us be willing to lead it! I will never forget the way the humility of that trusting request for prayer struck me in that moment. How were they able, I wondered in myself, to find in themselves the courage to cross that invisible, malignant line that divided our two groups to ask for what they needed from us, who, without really meaning to, even now kept ourselves so sadly separate? Were they enabled to come to us by the gratitude and attention with which Nicole and John had been receiving their stories of Stefan? Or were they like one Abba in the ancient Egyptian desert who was said to be like God on earth, because he covered the sins of the world as though he didn't see them?[3] I don't know.

What I do know, however, is this: When the lot fell on me to lead the prayer, I was overwhelmed, first, with a sudden knowledge of my own stiff-necked failure before now to acknowledge the extent of the suffering and goodness of Stefan's friends and their loyalty to him. Second, in that moment of repentance, I was overcome with a terrible, blessed rush of humility and gratitude that, in spite of my own hitherto unrecognized arrogance toward them, in their request they—and God in them—had come to me and to all of us to give us exactly what it was we needed. And how very much they had to give to us, so hungry as we were to share in the broken bread of the invisible Eucharist they offered now!

So, together, we pushed the heavy black chairs into an enormous circle, and together we sat—grieving long-haired, tattooed friends of Stefan's in heavy boots and buckles and pierced body parts, interspersed with grieving

---

3. Macarius the Great 32, *Sayings of the Desert Fathers*, trans. Ward, p. 134.

middle-class women and men in conventional hair and jewelry and clothing. Tightly, we held one another's hands.

I began our prayer by asking for God's comfort and help for Stefan and his family and for all of us who were there for them. After that, all those men and women who were so inclined recalled and thanked God for the things Stefan did and was for which they were most grateful. How very true and full of grace were the words that followed! I will never forget the sense I had in that moment that not only Stefan's life but my life and all of our lives were held in existence by the directness, love, and goodness of the prayers of Stefan's friends.

At the end of this time of testimony we prayed again for the easing of Stefan's pain and recited the Lord's Prayer together; after that, we sat in silence holding hands for a little while more, and said "Amen."

Then, all of a sudden one of Stefan's friends cried out. "I'm not finished!" he said. He looked around the enormous circle beseechingly. "We want Stefan to live! We need to pray for a miracle!"

My stomach turned over. How could there be a miracle now? Stefan's organs were already too deteriorated for there to be any hope that he would live. What would happen to the innocence of these people with their earnest faith when Stefan died? I looked around the circle at the nodding heads. Who was I, in my own arrogance, to refuse? I opened the prayers again, and this time a few of Stefan's friends poured out to God their tears, their grief, and their longing that, in spite of everything, Stefan might still live.

At the end of this second series of prayers, Stefan's friends were satisfied. Shortly after that they formed a quiet line and went to Stefan's room one by one to say good-bye. When they came out they stood for a while in the hall and in the waiting room in little groups; a few sat back down to wait, including the one-eyed man on crutches whom I was able to talk to later in the evening. Most of the rest said good-bye to John and Nicole, Christopher and Laurie, and left.

At eleven-thirty some of us, including Richard and I, said good-bye to John and Nicole and went home; we had said our good-byes earlier to Stefan. At four-thirty Tuesday morning Elaine called to say that Stefan had died, his family around him.

The next day Nicole told me of seeing him for the last time. The nurse had asked them to leave the room while he unhooked Stefan from the machinery that had kept him alive. When they had come back to the room, one of his friends was already there, softly playing "Knocking on Heaven's Door" on his guitar. Stefan was beautiful; he no longer looked injured. Finally, he was at peace. The friend suggested that they hold hands and recite the Lord's Prayer together, and as they prayed, he played again softly and comforted them a little.

The memorial service took place the following Saturday. Nicole and John wanted it to be a Eucharist planned and celebrated by the community of their friends, as we celebrate it in Emmaus. At the same time, it was important to Stefan's family—as it was to all of us who had been so touched by them—that the service be one in which Stefan's friends had a central place.

More than four hundred people were at the service, filling the balconies of the chapel and spilling out into the hall. It began with twenty-six people, friends and family, carrying candles, one for each year of Stefan's life, to place on the altar beside the many mementos of his childhood and the gifts left in Stefan's room in the hospital along with the beautiful yellow shirt. The last person who left his offering was the one-eyed man on crutches.

For the gospel, the beatitudes as they are found in Matthew were read. It was strange to me how, after struggling all my life to make sense of them, suddenly they seemed to be only an infinitely moving factual description of what I had just spent a week witnessing for myself. "Blessed are the poor in spirit. . . . Blessed are those who mourn, for they shall be comforted. Blessed are the humble. . . . Blessed are those who hunger and thirst for righteousness. . . . Blessed are the pure in heart, for they shall see God." They were about Stefan and his friends.

After that came the time when whoever chose could come up to the front and speak. Many did, and of them all, three especially stand out for me. The first, who struck me by his care of Nicole and John, was a pony-tailed, black-leather-jacketed man of about forty. He told of meeting Stefan through his eleven-year-old daughter fifteen years earlier. Not knowing he was the girl's father, whenever Stefan had seen him, Stefan had greeted him, "Hey dude, whatcha doing?" Then, one day Stefan discovered he was his friend's father, not just some older guy who hung out at her house. "After that, it was nothing but 'yes sir; no sir!' " The man paused as he told it, then turned to speak to Nicole and John directly. "All this reminds me of Matthew 7:20, where it says, 'by their fruits you shall know them,' " he said. "What Stefan was like tells me what you are like; he was so polite and so generous and kind and he had this rare gift of being able to make people feel good about things. My life would never have been the same without Stefan. I want to thank you for being his parents. God bless you," he added before he sat down.

The second person, whose unromantic, infinitely valuable truthfulness about Stefan stands out for me, was that of a large bald-headed man in a checked suit with a white shirt and skinny tie. He had worked with Stefan off and on for many years as a bouncer in a club. He began by speaking painfully and directly to Stefan of their friendship—"the things we did together; I'll always thank you for that." He concluded by stating earnestly and to much laughter, "Stefan was a good man; he never did anything to anyone unless he deserved it!"

The last speaker whose testimony I particularly re-member was a forty-something former wrestler named Arlo. He, too, began by speaking of his good times with Stefan, and his sadness, but he concluded that "the same God who gave life also created death, and so we will grieve and miss him, but Stefan has gone on to a better place." This time, hearing that trite old expression in the context of the hard life Stefan had led over the past ten years, I thought that he spoke the truth.

At the end of the testimonies, Richard and Betsy led us in the Eucharist we had already been living out implicitly all that week. Over the bread and wine we prayed the prayers for Easter we use in Emmaus, saying:

We remember how when we ourselves were dead and
    buried in the pain of betrayals and memories,
    in the wounds of sorrow and the sleep of sin,
    in the abandonment of death,
you did not leave us to destruction,
but you came among us as one of us, entering the very
    ocean of our death and suffering,
    to raise us up with you through those dreadful
    waters to new life.
In you, the joy of the resurrection renews the whole
    world,
    bringing hope where there is no hope,

> covering the dry ground with growing things,
> healing our mortal wounds of sorrow,
> bringing life to our dead hearts.

Together, we said the Lord's Prayer; together, we ate and drank. Friends of Stefan's sang two songs they had written for him, I played my flute, and the service was over. Except for the wonderfully crowded reception that followed it, the week of Stefan's death was over, too.

❈ ❈ ❈ ❈ ❈ ❈ ❈ ❈ ❈ ❈ ❈ ❈ ❈ ❈ ❈ ❈ ❈ ❈ ❈ ❈ ❈ ❈ ❈ ❈ ❈ ❈ ❈ ❈ ❈ ❈ ❈ ❈ ❈ ❈ ❈ ❈ ❈

Now, my friend, having told my story, and thinking once again of the questions around prayer and healing we were discussing at the beginning of this letter, I can hear you asking me, "In all these terrible events around Stefan's death and funeral, tell me what it was exactly that you found you needed healing from, and how was it that you found it?"

What invisible thing was it in me that needed healing? The long and the short of it is this: Ever since I began to learn from and be blessed by the monastic teachers of the ancient Egyptian desert, I had been convinced that there is almost nothing more destructive to the self and to the love of others than judgmentalism. Theodore of Pherme, one of those teachers, used to say, "There is no other virtue than that of not being scornful,"[4] and I had

---

4. Theodore of Pherme 13, *Sayings of the Desert Fathers*, trans. Ward, p. 75.

thought I believed it and tried to practice it with my whole heart. Once I found myself really confronted by Stefan and his friends, it was devastating to discover myself to be so full of scorn toward them that I had written them all off as leading lives of no consequence and—dare I say it?—of being worthless people.

How could I so have gone against what I professed to believe? I was able to do it, first, because I shared so deeply and so automatically in my own culture, which values not just work but a certain kind of work and productivity, not just stability but a certain kind of stability. I was also, however, encouraged to dismiss the lives of Stefan and his friends because of my own anxieties around loss and my own need for stability and fears of instability that stem not from my Christian values but from my childhood experiences.

What God did for me, the prayer God gave me, to use Evagrius' expression, was to hold my contempt, my unconscious sense of superiority and fear of all forms of loss before me so that I could see myself in it as in a mirror. Then, in the place of my contempt, God showed me God's name hallowed in Stefan's life and the lives of Stefan's friends, by the solidity, depth, and goodness of the love they gave to one another, but also to the rest of us, as well.

At the same time, God made it clear to me how it could have been that the Pharisees (of whom I am one by profession), holding on to their own ideas of righteousness, would have rejected Jesus, while those like Stefan and his friends who lived "unclean" lives of hardship and instability on the fringes of society accepted him with joy. Where in the gospels does Jesus praise my own desired middle-class stability? "Foxes have holes in the ground, but the Son of Man has no place to lay his head." "Let the dead bury the dead." For the sake of the kingdom, let me sell it all and buy instead the pearl of great price, the treasure in the field!

So am I really "healed" of my scorn? I would like to think I am, but I know too much from my own experience and from my monastic teachers to believe it. These wounded states of mind, heart, and perception that they call the passions have roots too deep to be weeded out all at once. Rather, pulling out the weeds is the prayer work of a lifetime. Still, what I also believe is that next time the temptation to scorn arises, I will not be taken so much by surprise. Where I wasn't even aware of its presence before, now, at least, I watch for it in my own heart, ready to fight against it. And knowing what I know now, if I give in to it, it will be a sin.

Before I close this letter, let me share with you one more thing I've been thinking about in connection with the kind of prayer and healing we've been talking about. It has to do with the role and place of gratitude.

When I look back over that time in the hospital and in the days that followed, what seems to mark them all is a blessed gratitude to Nicole and John for letting me share in what was happening to them; to the people at the hospital for their competence and careful kindness; to the members of my community for their love toward one another and desire to share the burden of Stefan's family's pain; to Stefan's friends for their willingness to cross the invisible lines, tell us who Stefan was, and pray; and to God, who underlaid everything and everybody with generous goodness and made us one.

But what was this all-pervasive gratitude? I think, before this, I had always thought of it as a kind of virtue that we work at developing, a proper acknowledgment that I owe because someone—God or mortal—has done something for me. Now gratitude seems very different to me. It is not something we do at all. Rather, it is a medium of grace, a gift of God that softens the heart and enables it to see and hear and receive the things that come to it from God. Like the perfume Mary poured over the feet of Jesus, like the yellow shirt left in Stefan's room by his friend, it is the extravagant expression of the bounty of divine and human love that bears all things, believes all things, hopes all things, and endures all things. If it is God who gives prayer, then God often gives it in the form of gratitude, and gratitude itself, when it is received attentively in prayer, is healing to the heart. Prayer is such a mysterious business for something so ordinary and everyday.

Know that I keep you ever in my heart.

*Roberta*

# Tree in the Forest, Tree in the Field: Mysteries

*My dear friend,*

In the light of all you and I have been seeking in our prayer, and in the light of our very desire to do that seeking, you asked me in your last letter what I think is in us that draws us toward God. Is it something that is a part of all human beings by nature or is it something that comes to us from our culture? Is it something innate, you wonder? What is it, precisely, that we are looking for? Is it something we learn, and if it is, how is it that we learn it?

How much time I have spent over the years pondering these very mysteries myself! Philosophers, sociologists, anthropologists, historians of religion, psychologists, and theologians have written enough books over the years on just this subject to supply an army of seekers with reading matter for the next twenty years. Still, I am aware that you aren't asking me for a summary of their opinions; you yourself know them better than I do. You are asking for what I myself think, so I will have to oblige you the best I can.

Let me start by stating the obvious: Most of what I know about anything complex relating to prayer I know from the way the theology and practice of the early church I study intersects with my own experience, prayer, and theological reflection, and this is surely the case with respect to these questions, too. As usual, I believe we can talk about complicated divine and human things best if, rather than starting with neat, sleek theories of the way things are, we begin with actual messy, ambiguous stories. Once having told the stories, we will be in a position to try to make sense of them. All this being true, you will not be surprised if I answer your questions by telling you two true stories. After that, I will reflect on each of them in the light of what I have learned from my own early church teachers.

\* \* \* \* \* \* \* \* \* \* \* \* \* \* \* \* \* \* \* \* \* \* \* \* \* \* \* \* \* \* \* \* \* \* \* \* \* \* \* \* \* \* \* \*

"Do you believe in predestination or free will?" my uncle Quentin asked my great-aunt Nacky.

Forgotten by Uncle Quentin and Aunt Nacky in the front seat, I was lying down flat and quiet on the back seat of Aunt Nacky's new pale blue, four-door 1949

Plymouth. In my white piqué skirt my mother had made me and my blue ruffled halter I tensed my body and held my breath to hear her answer. I was nine years old, and my mother, my little brothers, and I were paying our annual visit from New York City to my grandparents' farm in Union County, Kentucky.

Tonight Aunt Nacky, Uncle Quentin, and I were coming home from the fourth evening service of the yearly revival at Pond Fork Baptist Church, my family's white frame church close to the Big Ditch, out by Uncle Bob and Aunt Ida's house. Uncle Quentin was driving. Uncle Quentin was my mother's youngest brother, and he was home for the summer before he entered law school at the University of Kentucky in the fall. I liked Quentin. Not being quite a grown-up himself, I wasn't as afraid of him as I was of other grown-up people, and furthermore, he was funny.

As for Aunt Nacky, I didn't like her; I adored her. She was my grandmother's eccentric, dramatic, exuberant third sister, and she had a way with children. Aunt Nacky had taught the second-grade class at Sturgis Elementary School for thirty years, and so she was loved not just by me, but by just about every man, woman, and child over the age of seven in Union County. Still, all this being true, she was not a good driver. Every year Aunt Nacky would wreck a different new car against the same inconveniently placed tree at the side of this very road. This was why Quentin was driving. My mother had me ride back to my grandmother's with Aunt Nacky only on the condition that someone else drove.

Tonight, however, I myself had certainly not been paying attention to anybody's driving. Looking up out the window into the darkness of the murky summer sky, I was only barely aware of the flat, crunching sound of the tires on the newly oiled gravel road, or the sound of cicadas' sighing songs rising and falling like breathing. As we passed through the July fields of corn and hay and cattle, I hardly noticed the musky odors of animals wild and tame, the sharp scents of weeds and crops, or even the funny, closed-in smell of the scratchy woolen upholstery on which I lay.

What I was doing there in the back seat instead was some very heavy theological thinking. I was sorting through what I knew about God, about faith and its contents, and whether I had what it took to be saved. It was panicky, painful work I had never done before.

Up till this summer I had loved everything about going with my great aunts to Pond Fork Baptist Church. The old building, with its scuffed-up floor, hard wooden benches, potbellied stove, and high windows, was beautiful to me. I thought it wonderful to attend Sunday school classes in the funny upstairs rooms made by dividing off sections of the narrow balcony with long beige curtains.

I had loved the children's programs. Vacation Bible school always ran concurrently with the revival, and even this morning I had enjoyed there such pleasures as listening to my great-aunt Ginny's weird explanations of standard Bible stories, making cross-shaped book-ends out of plaster of Paris, and during refreshment time, eating the soft country sugar cookies and drinking the little paper cups of red Kool-Aid.

I had been unprepared tonight at the revival, how-ever, when everything changed, because I had loved the worship services, too, even the boring parts. I hadn't expected it when what I had already heard without harm a thousand times before in that place caught me and entangled me. Now I was scared to death.

The sweltering July evening had started off normally for a revival. The mothers and older ladies fanned themselves as always with their Whitsel Brothers Fu-neral Home fans. There had been the usual prayers for God's reviving and cleansing Spirit interspersed with dramatic hymns about blood and scripture readings about judgment.

Then Brother Smith had begun his message. He had taken for his text the story of the rich fool who had torn down his barns to build them bigger. The preacher had begun by retelling the story in detail, reminding us of how the barn builder had not only forgotten that if God were in the right mood for it, he could and would knock down dead any unprepared, unrepentant, unbelieving man, woman, or little girl who struck his fancy. The barn builder had also tried to get away with not tithing to his church.

I was already scared, but the preacher was just getting started. From there, making use of a lot of hard shouting and whispering and quoting of scripture, Brother Smith had tried to convince his little congregation of hard-working farmers, worn-out women, and wiggling children that, worse than the barn builder, every one of them was also a sinner wallowing in sins, secret and open. Their sins—our sins—were disbelief, disobedience to God, swearing, drinking, adultery (What was adultery? I hoped it was the sort of thing having to do with adults that somebody was always telling me I would understand when I was older, rather than something I didn't know I was already committing), playing cards, smoking, coveting, bearing false witness, and lack of faith.

After a whole lot of this, Brother Smith got to the three-pronged conclusion he was aiming at all along. His first point went something like this: Because we were all such hopeless sinners, every one of us was deserving of the fierce hell and the cruel devil that were waiting opened-mouthed below us, and indeed, this was precisely what was going to happen to practically everybody. God intended us, predestined us, for hell, and we were going there, and that was all there was to it. The congregation groaned. Somebody yelled out, "God for-bid!"

Next, Brother Smith came to his second point. Upon some people, he whispered, upon some of the lucky few who were present in that very room, God might have infinite mercy, not because they were good, "for all had sinned and come short of the glory of God," but because God had simply decided to save them, had predestined them to salvation. At this, a sprinkling of "Lord-a-mercy"s and "tell it, brother"s rose above the groans.

Finally, while the congregation moaned in the back-ground, a sweating Brother Smith reached the conclu-sion he'd been building to all evening. Even for those whom in his infinite mercy God had decided to rescue, he told us now, there was only one way we might claim it: we must "repent and believe the Good News of Jesus Christ"; we must believe that God loved us and "take Jesus for our personal Lord and savior."

Soon after that the preacher had announced the altar call and the congregation leaned back from the edge of the benches, every head bowed and every eye closed, to begin to sing "Softly and Tenderly Jesus Is Calling." Wrung out, they waited for the sound of footsteps on the wooden floor announcing either that someone had been scared enough to come forward for the first time to confess the name of Jesus, or that someone else had been terrorized once again into rededicating his or her life to him.

Though I was frightened nearly out of my mind, I knew myself to belong to neither category. Leaning forward with my face in my hands on the old wooden pew between Great-aunt Nacky and Great-aunt Ginny, I had repented and repented in great waves of stomach-wrenching fear, as though I were throwing up. "Believe!" the preacher had shouted, and I had believed. I had believed every single bit of the Bad News of Jesus Christ without question, about my sinfulness, about my death, which I knew was as likely to come on me at an unexpected moment as the barn builder's had been to come on him, and about God's terrible, waiting, predestined judgment.

What I couldn't believe was the rest. Gritting my teeth and trying as I might, I couldn't believe God loved me; I couldn't believe God wanted to save me; and I couldn't believe that I could believe. With my nine-year-old hands over my nine-year-old face, I combed out my heart with a lice-comb for a single sign that I believed could save me, but I found nothing. I knew I was among the damned.

At the end of the last prayer when everybody got up to leave, I could hardly stand up. My knees shook with terror, and the inside of my mouth was as dry as a rag. I hung on to my great-aunt Nacky for dear life. I needed her. I needed her to tell me something about the gospel that I'd missed or I hadn't understood that could make me believe. I needed her to save me from the wrath of hell.

But how was I going to get from her what I needed? Not by my asking her or any other grown-up directly, that's for sure. Back home in New York, religion wasn't something I could ask questions about. Talk about religion wasn't forbidden, exactly, but in terms of the effect of its discussion on the household, it came close to it. When the topic did come up, my cynical, charming, intelligent, perfectionistic, and authoritarian New Yorker father (whom I admired, loved, and feared) told his stories designed to illustrate how all organized religion was a racket, how all preachers, priests, and ministers were on the take, and how fools who believed a single thing they said got what they deserved.

My father's stories upset my mother and put her in a bad place with respect to us. I could see that she didn't want us to hear what he said and that she certainly didn't want us to ask either her or him about it, because on principle she wouldn't disagree with my father even if he had said sweet was salty and salty, sweet. Furthermore, I was no dummy. I knew that she had been raised in the very Pond Fork Baptist Church where I had just had the wits scared out of me. I always figured she had to believe what they preached. I had no reason to think she had questions about God and faith and hell and sin or the other things I was worrying about, either. She would think me bad, I believed, for having the doubts, and bad for rocking the boat in the family by asking questions, besides.

As for my churchgoing family in Union County, Kentucky, I couldn't ask any of them, either, not even Aunt Nacky. It seemed clear to me that even to suggest to my grandmother or my great-aunts that I had some of the questions I had would tell them in a flash that I "didn't have faith," and that therefore I wasn't saved. On top of that, a lot of my boy cousins already laughed at me for being and talking like a Yankee. I couldn't stand my own potential humiliation, or their pity and scorn in the face of my unbelief, either.

So this is why, lying in Aunt Nacky's back seat, I was going through everything Pond Fork Baptist had taught me about belief and salvation.

So far, halfway between Pond Fork and my grand-mother's farm, the prospect looked bad. I had just reminded myself that, though I believed in the Ten Commandments at one level (Aunt Ginny had had us memorize them on Tuesday at Bible school), at another level I didn't at all because I didn't keep them. Although I tried to "do the right thing," and indeed, longed with all my heart to be good, I never succeeded. With my father, especially, I was always in trouble for disobedi-ence, and I knew that this was the same as disobedience to God. I was afraid of my father, and so I regularly bore false witness by lying to him. I felt terrible that my room at home was a mess, that I lost my sweaters everywhere, that I was greedy and selfish, and that my perpetually unfinished homework was covered with smears and wrinkles, but I couldn't seem to do better no matter how hard I tried. For these things it was clear that the least I deserved was hell.

Still, I knew that if I could repent enough for these things and stop doing them, God would forgive me. But there were two more categories of sins that appeared hopeless because, try as I might, I really couldn't keep myself from committing them. The first of them had to do with what as an adult I would now call dispositions and attitudes and even virtues. The nine-year-old child I was would have called them feelings.

A lot of time was spent at Pond Fork reminding everybody of what they already knew about acceptable and unacceptable states of mind for Christians. On the positive side, that it was necessary to love and forgive everyone, of course, for which trust and obedience to God were essential. These virtues and dispositions were well illustrated in two of Pond Fork's favorite hymns, " 'Tis So Sweet to Trust in Jesus" and "Trust and Obey." Anger, above all, but also selfishness and disobedience figured prominently on the negative side.

As I lay in the back seat of Aunt Nacky's Plymouth, I knew I was in trouble when I thought just about my anger. I remembered my struggles against my continual anger at my human and my heavenly fathers. I might be a sinner, but I hated the way they bossed me around, broke me, judged me, and dismissed me as though I were worth nothing to them. I also considered how, no matter how hard I tried not to be, I was angry at most of the other adults in my life, too, as well as at my little brother, Fred. Jesus was very clear that Christians are to love both God and their neighbors as themselves, but most of the time I was too angry or too hurt to feel very loving, so the prospect of my salvation looked pretty hopeless here, too.

It was only, however, when I considered the third category of sin I couldn't seem to help committing no matter how hard I tried, that I really did decide it must be hopeless. This third type of sin had to do with my across-the-board inability to "only believe" that the things grown-ups told me were true. You must understand that these unbelievable things were not all overtly religious in content. For example, at home, my mother told me I must believe that it hurt my father to punish me; at school, my teacher told us we must believe that no bombs would ever be dropped on P.S. 41, although we had air-raid drills regularly to protect us against the threat of the Russian atomic bombs the radios were full of. Good children were supposed to believe what they were told against the evidence of their senses; if we said that we couldn't, we were punished.

At Pond Fork Baptist Church, the things I was told I must believe were mostly religious things, and they were of three kinds. The first had to do with the Bible. I was to admit that everything written in the Bible happened exactly the way the Bible said it did—the stories in the Old Testament of Adam and Eve, the parting of the Red Sea, and Jonah being swallowed by the whale. In the New Testament I was to believe in Jesus' miracle stories, that Jesus was God, that God would give you anything you prayed for if you had the faith of a mustard seed, that Jesus rose from the dead, heaven after death, that all people are sinners, and most important of all, in the Second Coming and the Last Judgment.

Try as hard as I could, except for the parts about my being a sinner and the Last Judgment and hell, which I always found totally plausible, I could hardly believe any of it. It was too much for my common sense. I simply couldn't stop myself from knowing that nobody had been around at the creation of the world to report what had happened, that I had never seen a miracle, and that no one had actually ever come back from the dead to say if there is a heaven or hell at all.

The second group of things I had to believe about God were easier in some ways, harder in others. I was to believe that God was our father, like my own father but bigger and even more exacting. Though I only half believed it, it was plausible. In the face of human failure, God the father was "righteous, just and good"; God hated sin and was angry at my failures and imperfections. This was also believable. God was all-powerful but he loved me; he would unfailingly punish me unless I acknowledged that he loved me enough to make his own son die in my place, and I was to love him for it in return. At least this was plausible.

The third, and really nonnegotiable sticker was this: I was to believe that the human Jesus was both the only son of God and "the *only* way to the father," and that unless a person believed in Jesus alone, that person was damned. This one I couldn't believe no matter how hard I tried. Just that year I had been to the Metropolitan Museum with my fourth-grade class. How could I make myself not know that throughout history most people— Egyptians, Greeks, Romans, Hindus, Buddhists—over the history of the world were not Christian? I had seen the statues of their gods and goddesses with my own eyes. I couldn't help knowing that all those other people believed in their gods and goddesses at least as firmly as I was being ordered to believe. How could the folk at Pond Fork Baptist Church think that they were right and all those other people and their civilizations for all those centuries were wrong? What kind of God would condemn all those people to hell just for believing things they thought were true?

It was just then, as I lay there mulling despairingly over this last question, that my uncle Quentin's young lawyer's voice broke the stuffy silence of Aunt Nacky's light blue '49 Plymouth.

"Aunt Nack," Quentin said, "do you believe in free will or predestination?"

Quentin had read my mind. It was the very question I was getting to, myself. I held my breath and lay perfectly still, to hear what Aunt Nacky would say.

Aunt Nacky took the question seriously, so she didn't answer it at once, but when she did, she went right to the heart of what I needed to know.

"Free will or predestination?" Aunt Nacky said. "I guess human beings have the choice of whether they will be ornery or not, but I surely don't think the good Lord wants any of his children to go to hell, whatever that old Brother Smith might say. People are saved more ways than one." She paused and thought about it all a little longer, then she went on. "I reckon God knows most of us are just about doing the best we can do most of the time, anyway."

The sob that had been searing the walls of my chest for the last hour began to subside. I was not going to hell, after all. I waited for more, but Quentin didn't reply and Aunt Nacky didn't say anything else.

For now, I would be all right. Though by morning the fear of God and the anger of the adults in my life who never believed I was doing my best would tear at me again with their burning teeth, for now, I knew without a shadow of a doubt that what Aunt Nacky had just said was true, and it was enough. It would get me through the night.

\* \* \* \* \* \* \* \* \* \* \* \* \* \* \* \* \* \* \* \* \* \* \* \* \* \* \* \* \* \* \* \* \* \* \* \* \* \* \* \* \* \*

So what about it? Was the religious impulse of that little girl, Roberta, learned or innate? It seems to me now that, on the surface, and maybe deep down, too, the bulk of what motivated her in her religious life, as well as the precise shape and form of it, was not just learned, it was deliberately taught. How hard they had worked, those teachers, preachers, and deacons at Pond Fork Baptist Church, to convey to her not just the content of what they understood the Christian faith to be, but also the desire for it! How carefully they taught her not just what the Bible said, but how a person's heart should be situated with respect to it! With what attention did they fill her sleep with dreams of judgment, fear of God, and a longing to be found acceptable not just by God but by the universe itself! How hard her father had worked to establish his authority over her, to teach her to fear him for her own good, to get her to believe absolutely what he told her, and to destroy what he thought of as her potential gullibility in all areas of religion!

And they were very successful. I learned at Pond Fork what I was supposed to learn. I learned well, too, what my father intended to teach me, and I, dangling in awful anguish above the fires of hell, was caught between them.

What finally saved me at that time, not from the fires of hell, but rather from total and absolute despair, however, was nothing of this. It was what I was able to learn, entirely by accident in the back seat of Aunt Nacky's Plymouth, of another, truer and more life-giving way of seeing who God is and how God sees human beings in return. That I learned these new things was and is a mystery. No one intended to teach me what I learned that night; in fact, Aunt Nacky wouldn't even have said what she did if she had thought I was listening.

Even more mysterious to this very day, however, is not so much *that* I learned it, but rather, how it was that I both *wanted* to learn and was *able* to learn—not just to hear but to *believe* what Aunt Nacky said, to know without a shadow of a doubt that what she said was true. How could I possibly have known that her words were true when I heard her speak them? Surely they contradicted not only everything I had explicitly been told; they contradicted almost all of my experience as well. So, in spite of all this, how did I know the truth, the good truth when I heard it?

I believe now that it was because in my heart there *was* an innate, God-given yearning for God that allowed me to know it. But the question of what this religious impulse is still remains.

Augustine, the great African Christian Platonist theologian of the fifth century, begins his long autobiographical prayer *The Confessions* with a reflection on what it means to be human. ["Oh God,"] he prays, "you have made us for yourself, and our hearts are restless till they find their rest in you."[1] Augustine would have had no problem explaining what had happened to me: it was my innate yearning for God that saved me.

But what is this yearning about, and what does a yearning for God have to do with the back seat of Aunt Nacky's snazzy car? As a Christian Platonist, Augustine was convinced that *all* things that exist are related to God in such a way that they only are able to become what they actually are meant to be by a primeval, mindless yearning toward God, who draws them to God's self to become what they are meant to be by God's own yearning toward them. It is this that makes lions able to act like lions, not earthworms, and acorns grow into oak trees, not rhubarb. An odd idea, isn't it? In a special way, human beings, too, being made in the image of God, only become real human beings, are only able

---

1. *Confessions,* I.1. trans. R. S. Pine-Coffin (New York: Penguin Classics, 1961), p. 21.

to grow and thrive as human beings as they also yearn for God.

Christian Platonists, and non-Christian Platonists, too, for that matter, suggest that in human beings there are three parts to this innate, God-given yearning for God. The first is a longing for *goodness, for God who is good,* but also—and here is the really important part of this—because we are made in the image of God's goodness, it is a longing that we ourselves be good. Sometimes, many times, because of the presence of sin in our world, human beings get confused about what that goodness actually is, and inadvertently we want terrible things and do terrible things as a result, but this doesn't destroy the point. It is goodness that even twisted human beings desire because they are made that way. I believe it was this desire for goodness, human and divine, all mingled with a fear of hell and a wish to please, that motivated that child in the car as she lay, assessing what she had been taught, trying to find for herself a way into life and not death.

This, of course, wasn't the whole of it. According to our Christian Platonist teachers, the second part of the yearning for God is a longing for *truth, for God is truth.* You may not be surprised to find out that, just as in the case of goodness where there is a correspondence between God's goodness and human goodness, there is also a correspondence between God's truth and human truth. That is, because we are made in the image of God, human beings are endowed with an innate ability that predisposes them to want and need the truth to thrive, to try to come to true explanations for how things are, and to recognize the truth when they meet it. This gift, this second part of the religious impulse, this desire for the truth and the ability to know it when she saw it, I believe is what enabled the child who was me, in the face of all contrary learning, to recognize that what Aunt Nacky had said was true.

Still, these—the desire for goodness and the desire for truth—are only two of the three parts of the innate religious impulse, the yearning for God that Christian Platonists teach us about. Before I speak of the third, let me tell you another story about the same child.

\* \* \* \* \* \* \* \* \* \* \* \* \* \* \* \* \* \* \* \* \* \* \* \* \* \* \* \* \* \* \* \* \* \* \* \* \* \* \*

It was a bitter October a year and a half later, the kind of month that ended with a Halloween so cold that we had to wear coats over our ghost and fairy princess costumes when we went trick-or-treating. That fall I would turn eleven. I had taken one more summer trip to Union County, attended one more vacation Bible school, and one more terrifying revival. Now, back in New York City where I lived the rest of the year, I had begun to attend a confirmation class with a handful of other sixth graders. It met on Thursday afternoons at Christ the King Lutheran Church not too far from where I lived.

What I was doing in that class I scarcely remember. Surely, my summer stints at Pond Fork Baptist Church had given me a painfully avid interest in God, sin and judgment, and the meaning of life, mine in particular, compared to that of most of the other sixth graders I knew. But I also recall that we children were an ecumenical lot in those days in Oakland Gardens apartments where I lived. Perhaps I had asked my mother to let me go with a girl I knew from there. God knows, Mother, with a new baby in the house, would have been glad to have me gone one afternoon a week. Still, I can't recall attending Lutheran church services, and there have never been any Lutherans in our family on either side. I wasn't actually confirmed there because we had moved to Delaware by Christmas.

Whatever the reasons, I do recall that I wanted to go. The classes were held on the second floor of the back of the fortress-like gray stone church, in a little dark cream-colored room with a green linoleum floor, small casement windows on two sides, and a lightbulb hanging at the end of a naked wire from the ceiling. There was a fireplace that didn't work on one of the outside walls; the fireplace was topped with a carved gray stone mantel too narrow to set anything on it. On one of the inside walls there was a large dented floor lamp that stood beside a picture of a wavy-haired Jesus who was on his knees, submissively looking upward toward his father with more innocence than I could ever hope to muster.

In the middle of the room, there were two large, scuffed library tables surrounded by the straight-backed wooden chairs in which we learned, and the shabby armchair with its flowered slipcover from which the pastor taught.

I remember that there were eight of us in the class, six girls and two boys. I can recall a fair amount about the sly and awkward boys. Both had straight brown hair, slicked back and held in place with perfumed stickum. Both wore blue and brown button-up flannel shirts and brown oxfords, rather than the knit shirts and high-topped Bugs-Bunny-footed black and white sneakers of the boys in Oakland Gardens. I don't have much memory of the other five girls, except that they intimidated me with their insiders' giggles, their freshly combed hair, their clean white blouses, and their cardigan sweaters whose buttons never seemed to be lost.

As for the pastor himself, from the start I was afraid of him because he was a man, but also because he was a puzzle to me. He was an adult male like none other I had ever encountered. He wore black woolen suits with vests and white shirts and ties. His shoes were polished, and he spoke to us in the same authoritative, formal tone of voice that doctors and other men in authority used on children when they couldn't avoid speaking to them.

Still, for some reason I couldn't begin to fathom, he chose to spend an hour and a half a week with us children, the lowest of the low. Everybody knew that men after all, spent their time only with people worth talking to, and we were only boys and girls. I thought about it a lot. Maybe, I decided at last, it was not because the audience (us) was important to him, rather, it was his subject—religion, the Bible, and God—that was important.

I could understand his interest in teaching us religion, if this were true. Though the one I knew as God caused me great unhappiness, I longed for God, nonetheless, and religion was important to me. It gave me larger and more noble categories with which to try to understand the unhappiness of my life. It gave me a reason as well as a shape for the chaos and pain I felt. Like the fairy stories I loved to read, it gave me faint hope that someday I, too, might be the recipient of a miracle so that, in spite of my weakness and failure, I might be rescued, or even triumph on my own.

I vaguely remember the first two weeks of classes. Amidst the restless snickering and meaningful glances of the boys, we recited the Ten Commandments, and we learned to recite the Nicene Creed and answer the questions of the catechism. It was a lot like vacation Bible school and I was good at this sort of thing, but it didn't actually hold my interest any more than it held the other children's.

It was not until the third week, however, that Pastor Schmidt came up with an idea to try to perk us all up. At the end of the class, he announced a psalm memorizing contest. Each of us, he told us, was to choose a psalm on our own and memorize it. Whoever came back soonest with their psalm memorized would win an as yet unspecified prize. I was electrified. An exotic and mysterious prize! My greed was mobilized. I was determined to win it.

As soon as class was over, I ran back home to look in my closet, under my bed, and any place else I could think of for my old black Sunday school Bible. When I found it at last in a pile of blocks, I opened it up right at the first page of the book of Psalms. Psalm 1 looked short, so that was the one I decided to learn.

I worked at memorizing it all week in a frenzy of greed. I didn't think to care what it meant. "Blessed is the man who . . . ," I recited by rote while I ate my supper. "His delight is in the law of the Lord," I said to myself as I walked to school. "Who sitteth not in the seat of scorners," I mumbled in the bath under my breath. All through the weekend I worked away at it, wondering if, at that very moment, someone else in the class was drawing ahead of me in the race toward the prize.

Then, unexpectedly, sometime around Monday afternoon, as I was reciting verse 3 to myself, something happened. "He is like a tree, planted by a river of waters, which yields forth its fruit in its season. Its leaf also does not wither," I said to myself, and all of a sudden, I recognized this tree. It was a wonderful tree growing in the same mysterious forest the poor little princesses visited in my illustrated books of fairy tales. The tree was magical and beautiful, and the water it grew by was magical, too, hidden in a dark place full of moss that only I could find. Its fruit was precious, transparent, and colored like gemstones, and the deep forest sunlight glowed like fire as it passed through its never-withering leaves.

From that very moment, I knew that a beautiful, magical tree was not what the psalm was meant to be about, that there was even something not Christian about getting caught up in that forest of my imagination. Still, no matter how hard I fought against it, all the rest of the week, while I polished the last Bible verses right up through, "but the way of the wicked will perish," my fancy for the wonderful tree held me fast in its wicked grip, and I loved that tree with a guilty love.

Then, finally, it was Thursday. I climbed the back stairs almost more painfully excited than I could stand. Supposing everybody had their psalm memorized? How would Pastor Schmidt judge the contest then? My stomach ate into my back as he greeted us and called the roll.

At last he got down to what my every waking moment for the last week had been directed toward. "Has anyone got their psalm memorized yet?" he asked. My hand shot up; seven other pairs of eyes looked at the tabletop and seven mouths turned down at the corners. He turned to me, then. "Bobby Marie," he asked, "are you ready with your psalm?" I was. Trembling and halting, I recited it without a flaw.

Not really having expected anyone to have done it yet, Pastor Schmidt hadn't actually brought my prize, and after the first paralyzing disappointment wore off, the guilty frenzy in which I waited for it throughout the following week was greater than the frenzy in which I had memorized for it. What if he forgot it again? What if he didn't forget it, but it wouldn't be something I wanted? I hoped for crayons and a coloring book, or a fancy yo-yo, or a red rubber ball with a seam around it like the other girls had. In this way, I twisted myself up in anguish all that week. Still, at the very same time, the tree by the river of waters bowed down its lovely branches in its dark place in my mind and flourished.

The Wednesday night before the following Thursday I could hardly fall asleep for fear and excitement, and I woke up the next morning long before dawn. I learned nothing in school; my time that day was spent trying not to drown in the deep river that rushed between my guilty, seemingly pagan desire and my despairing fear that Pastor Schmidt would forget what had been promised to me, not just today, but for eternity.

Then, once again, it was Thursday afternoon, and this time the good pastor had indeed remembered to bring my prize. At the end of roll call, with great ceremony and a speech about the word of God, he handed me a little brown wrapped box. A pulse in my head was beating so hard and my hands were trembling so much that I could hardly take it from him. Embarrassed by the eyes of the other children, I unwrapped it slowly.

How can I describe to you what was in that box when I opened it at last? Never before or after, as a child or as an adult, have I received a present that so far outran my hopes for it. His gift exceeded my powers to describe it then, and it exceeds them, still.

Folded in its white nest of tissue paper, it was a most amazing tiny bottle of perfume. Its appearance alone enchanted me. The glass bottle itself was so clear that I could see the liquid inside it, but it was round and dimpled, exactly the texture of the skin of a real orange. The smooth cap was brown like a twig, and tied around its long neck with a white ribbon were two little red-centered white paper orange blossoms and a small white label with orange print that read "Souvenir of Florida." Florida!

I loved it as soon as I laid eyes on it. This love was nothing, however, to what came to me when my fumbling fingers unscrewed its tiny cap, and I raised the little bottle to my nose to smell its exotic scent. At once, in my amazed delight I recognized from whence this perfume had come. It was drawn from blossoms from my secret tree, the very tree of Psalm 1 that grew and flourished by the river of waters, the tree whose root never failed and whose leaf never withered. It was the tree of paradise; of course the scent of its flowers was beautiful! It was the smell of heaven, the very smell of God.

❊ ❊ ❊ ❊ ❊ ❊ ❊ ❊ ❊ ❊ ❊ ❊ ❊ ❊ ❊ ❊ ❊ ❊ ❊ ❊ ❊ ❊ ❊ ❊ ❊ ❊ ❊ ❊ ❊ ❊ ❊ ❊ ❊ ❊ ❊ ❊ ❊ ❊ ❊ ❊ ❊

How, then, did I recognize the scent I smelled for what it was? As I said, according to our ancient Christian Platonist teachers, by putting the gift of yearning for God into every human being's heart, God at the same time draws all people made in God's image to God's self and into their own true selves. As I have also said, the first two parts of this yearning for God are a longing for goodness and a longing for truth. The third part of this yearning is a saving longing for *beauty, for God who is goodness and truth is also beauty*. It is this innate human and divine longing, found in the company of goodness and truth, that is able to recognize and leap up at beauty and rejoice and know that all is beautiful, that there is not one speck of beauty under the sun that does not mirror back the beauty of God. This, I am sure, is the way that I recognized the odor of perfume for what it was, the scent of beauty, which is the smell of God.

But this still leaves the matter of whether there was any part of my ability to recognize the beauty of God that was actually not innate, and this is where it begins to get baffling. I learned, after all, so very little of what good, conscientious Pastor Schmidt had intended to teach me over the weeks of the confirmation class. I had known the Ten Commandments, and the contents of the catechism, too, long before we ever started, and I had known the rest of it from church and from reading the Bible story books my great-aunts in Union County sent me.

It is more significant to me that none of what he did teach me, or enabled me to learn, was deliberate; it appeared to be every bit inadvertent. No pastor, priest, or preacher would ever normally have given a child perfume as a prize in a Bible memorizing contest. Rather, I imagine now without any trouble how that Thursday more than forty years ago Pastor Schmidt remembered my gift only as he got up from the warm bed of his afternoon nap to come to our class.

"Mary Jane," he would have said to his wife as he tied his black wing-tips in a double knot, "it's time to go, and I've forgotten to get the Bible prize for that funny little girl I told you about. Could you look and see if you've got anything lying around that would do?"

"I'm sure I do," she would have answered, rummaging in the top drawer of her glass-topped dresser where she was already looking for her pink lipstick. "Here you are," she would have said a moment later as she drew out my little box. "Just let me put some paper on it for you."

Thus, I met up with the beauty of God.

❋ ❋ ❋ ❋ ❋ ❋ ❋ ❋ ❋ ❋ ❋ ❋ ❋ ❋ ❋ ❋ ❋ ❋ ❋ ❋ ❋ ❋ ❋ ❋ ❋ ❋ ❋ ❋ ❋ ❋ ❋ ❋ ❋ ❋ ❋ ❋

But oh, my friend, after all this, do I finally want to say that this movement toward God is learned or innate? As I look back over these two stories I just told you, and further back, not just back through the letters we have written to each other, but back through the whole of my life, it seems to me that the pieces of the answer come to me as transparent, as jumbled together, and most of all as mysterious as Florida orange blossom perfume made of the healing flowers of a magical tree from the forests of God.

Our yearning for God is learned. For some of us, it is partly learned in church or home, from nature and from scripture, from what we read and what we see. At least as much for some like us, however, it is learned in ways we never know from people, like my teachers at Pond Fork Baptist Church, my father, Aunt Nacky, and the Lutheran pastor and his wife, who teach us things they never intend to teach.

At the same time, this yearning is innate, part of the very image of God within us. Still, do not mistake what I mean; it is something more than blind instinct, something more than simple sense. It is a God-given turning of the appetite to the presence of God that grows continuously and bears its enchanted fruit in the dark forests of our deepest selves. At the same time, it is more than this. Do you remember the image of the field I told you of in my first letter all those months ago? For me, standing as I still do in that August field, drenched and happy in the cold rain, it is also a longing of the whole self for the ripening red apples of the ordinary presence of God, the apple tree.

What is this yearning? I think it is what we have been exchanging letters about, all along. It is prayer in all its infinite variety, the prayer we grit our teeth to pray and the prayer God gives that we hardly recognize as prayer at all. It is prayer as grace; no doing of our own, it is all mystery, all gift. It is prayer, the very face of God, God who once created us and who draws us into our own selves now, right straight through to the good, true, and beautiful self of God.

On this, I close. Watch and pray, my dear friend.

*Roberta*